POWER SHOP 6

Retail Design Now

FRAME

Content
POWERSHOP 6

BETTER TOGETHER – Retail space as a community forum

Interview	ALBERTO CAIOLA	6
Ædifica	JORDAN STORE	8
Alberto Caiola	HARBOOK	12
Barde + vanVoltt	SNEAKER DISTRICT	16
Batek Architekten	ZALANDO BEAUTY STATION	18
CBA Clemens Bachmann Architekten	ENOTHEK BRIENNER STRASSE	22
Curiosity	GINZA SIX	26
David Chipperfield Architects Milan	SSENSE MONTREAL	30
DFROST Retail Identity	ESSENCE MAKER SHOP	34
JSPR	FOUR BY AZZURO	38
Kapsimalis Architects	THE OPEN MARKET IN OIA	42
Knoblauch	SPORT FÖRG	46
Kokaistudios	NINGBO ALT-LIFE	48
Landini Associates	THE KITCHENS	52
Neri&Hu Design and Research Office	LITTLE B	56
Nike Design	NIKE HOUSE OF INNOVATION 000	60
Party/Space/Design	CHOCOLATE FACTORY	64
Schmidhuber	SIEMENS SHOWROOM	66
Studio Amber	WARRECORDS	68
Studio DLF	SLFT	72
Studio Roy de Scheemaker	SKINS COSMETICS	76
Studio XAG	NAPAPIJRI	80
UNStudio	LANE 189	84
UNStudio	TERMINAL 2 LANDMARK SPACE	88
Woods Bagot	OVER/UNDER KIOSKS	92

LET'S TALK ABOUT US – Retail space as a mirror of the brand

Interview	ALEX MOK AND BRIAR HICKLING	98
Archiee	EN	100
Area-17	JACOB COHËN	104
Atelier 522	ENGELHORN SPORTS	108
Brinkworth and Wilson Brothers	FIORUCCI	110
Burdifilek	MACKAGE	114
Christopher Ward Studio	OROVIVO 1856	118
Ciszak Dalmas Studio and Matteo Ferrari	MALABABA	122
Claudio Pironi & Partners	BILLIONAIRE	126
Corneille Uedingslohmann Architekten	KULT	130
Corneille Uedingslohmann Architekten	STUDIO JUSTE	134
Curiosity	MONCLER	136
Francesc Rifé	CAMPER	140
Ippolito Fleitz Group	HUNKE	144
Linehouse	HERSCHEL SUPPLY SHIBUYA	148
Masquespacio	DOCTOR MANZANA	152
Minas Kosmidis [Architecture in Concept]	NEW YORK SWEETS	154
MVRDV	BULGARI	158
Nong Studio	V2 BOUTIQUE	160
Ohlab	IN-SIGHT	164
Omer Arbel Office	HERSCHEL SUPPLY GASTOWN	168
Pattern Studio	THE DAILY EDITED	170
Schemata Architects	DESCENTE BLANC NAGOYA	174
Sergio Mannino Studio	GLAM SEAMLESS	178
Superfuturedesign*	MASEL	182
Tacklebox Architecture	CLAUS PORTO	186
Tchai	DHL EXPRESS	190
Zeller & Moye	TROQUER FASHION HOUSE	194

THE MEDIUM IS THE MESSAGE – Retail space as a storytelling device

Interview	GEORG THIERSCH	200
1zu33	AESOP NIKOLAISTRASSE	202
1zu33	PARFUMS UNIQUES	206
A Work of Substance	KHROMIS	210
Ædifica	MAISON BIRKS	214
Arket	004002 – 941	216
Bel Epok	SPITZENHAUS	220
CBA Clemens Bachmann Architekten	KOPPELMANN OPTIK	222
Christopher Ward Studio	ANIYE BY	224
Clou Architects	JEWELLERY BOX CHAOWAI	228
Creative Studio Unravel	IMMI	232
Do. Do.	ŌYANE SAIKAITOKI	236
Isora x Lozuraityte Studio for Architecture	FRIENDS & FRAMES	240
Kokaistudios	ASSEMBLE BY RÉEL	244
Landini Associates	GENTSAC	248
Landini Associates	SARAH & SEBASTIAN	250
Leckie Studio Architecture + Design	CHA LE MERCHANT TEAHOUSE	252
Linehouse	ALL SH	254
Marcante-Testa	IMARIKA	258
Moriyuki Ochiai Architects	CRYSTALSCAPE	262
RIGI Design	MAGMODE	266
Sergio Mannino Studio	MEDLY PHARMACY	270
Sid Lee Architecture	ADIDAS X CONCEPTS, THE SANCTUARY	274
Studio Malka Architecture	HOMECORE CHAMPS-ELYSÉES	278
Waterfrom Design	MOLECURE PHARMACY	282
Yagyug Douguten	BAKE CHEESE TART	286
Zentralnorden	SPOONING	290

THIS IS NOT JUST A CONSUMER GOOD – Retail space as a gallery

Interview	JOHANNES TORPE	294
Anagrama	NOVELTY	296
Brinkworth	BROWNS EAST	300
Brinkworth	BROWNS LA POP-UP	304
Burdifilek	MOOSE KNUCKLES	308
Calvi Brambilla	ANTONIOLUPI	312
CLOU architects	JIUXI WEDDING EXHIBITION	316
Curiosity	DOLCE & GABBANA	320
Diogo Aguiar Studio and Andreia Garcia Architectural Affairs	PRUDÊNCIO STUDIO	324
Eduard Eremchuk	GUAPA FLOWER SHOP	328
Eduard Eremchuk	LIKESHOP	332
Ito Masaru Design Project / SEI	ISAMU KATAYAMA BACKLASH	336
Johannes Torpe Studios	UNITED CYCLING	340
junya.ishigami+associates	JINS	344
Kengo Kuma & Associates	CAMPER	348
Maurice Mentjens	KIKI'S STOCKSALE	352
Montalba Architects	RAQUEL ALLEGRA	356
MVSA Architects	SHOEBALOO	360
Sibling Architecture	DOT COMME	364
Spacemen	BY	368
Studio David Thulstrup	TABLEAU FLOWER SHOP	372
Studio MK27	MICASA VOL.C	376
Superfuturedesign*	THE KAPE	380
Valerio Olgiati	CELINE	384
Index	DESIGNERS	388
Index	PROJECTS	398
Credits		400

BETTER TOGETHER

RETAIL SPACE AS A COMMUNITY FORUM

Interview

ALBERTO CAIOLA

Shanghai-based designer ALBERTO CAIOLA, winner of the Frame Award for Emerging Designer of the Year in 2019, expands on the benefits of bringing people together through meaningful experiences 'in a world where digital is becoming the new reality'.

What makes a successful retail space design? I believe there is not one strategy for all; every retailer will have to find their own unique path to engage with their clients and become attractive to other audiences. It is important that a wider connection is found that helps the brand communicate on a deeper emotional level. Design plays a role in this. Like music, it needs to take you somewhere else, to provide disruptive experiences and new sensations.

The blend of retail and hospitality is not a new trend, nor is the multi-purpose retail space. But more and more stores are moving a step further, into the realm of a community-building destination. Why do you think that is? The more we experience our globalised world through the lens of our screens, the more we need to exist in the physical world, to connect with people and share a sense of place. I believe we are increasingly missing a sense of identity which has to be found in communities and social ties in order to help us redefine our role in society.

Bringing people together in a call to action with positive values seems to me a great way to empower them and address a much needed sense of belonging.

What do you think is the main advantage and the main challenge of this approach to retail space design? As our lives become more driven by algorithms which are telling us what to do and what to buy, the idea of discovering something physically, through an unexpected shopping experience that surprises us becomes very appealing. Creating the opportunity for customers to connect with other people who are passionate and dedicated to a common interest further brings the brand alive, humanising it. This gives brands the chance to create a fan base or cultural club around an object, point of view or ideal.

The main challenge is to stay true to the brand's values while remaining relevant by generating new experiences.

We're seeing an ever-growing number of brick-and-mortar versions of online brands. Why are retail spaces still meaningful today? It stems from what I said above. As human beings, we will always need to exist within a community. Together with the promise to experience something new and meaningful, worth leaving the house for, this makes physical stores more meaningful than ever — in a world where digital is becoming the new reality.

What, in your opinion, is the main goal of retail spaces today, and how can interior design contribute to it? Online and offline are integrating each other. As online media is fulfilling the functions of stores — stock display, sales, etc. — stores are becoming media. They are no longer distributing products, but experiences. I believe our role as designers today is to develop successful frameworks for these experiences, in which brand stories can shine. Stores are territories to be explored, entertainment venues, cultural hubs, temples of enthusiasm to strongly support the values and the lifestyle or promises of the brand.

How do you envision the future of retail design? I picture it as a dynamic, immersive, multidimensional and visceral experience through a perfectly curated context.

'STORES ARE NO LONGER DISTRIBUTING PRODUCTS BUT EXPERIENCES'

Ill Ganger

Ædifica

JORDAN STORE

Basketball legends past and future rule the court in ÆDIFICA's slam dunk design

TORONTO — It was pretty much guaranteed that sneakerheads would flock to Nike's first Jordan Store in Canada, but as well as a successful retail location, Nike wanted to establish a thriving hub for Toronto's basketball community too. Designers Ædifica worked in close collaboration with the brand's creative teams, Set Creative and Foot Locker to 'create an immersive environment where brand identity, store experience and local pride would mesh.' In other words, somewhere that mixes Jordan swag with the city's talent.

Commercial activity is centred on the ground floor where a giant mural of Michael Jordan surveys large banks of sneakers and sportswear set against grey-painted brick walls, exposed concrete and steel. Anyone waiting to be served can have a go on the basketball hoop, which, thanks to modular display cases and flexible lighting, offers plenty of room for attempting a three-pointer. Local colour can be added in a customisation area where t-shirts and windbreakers can be adorned with neighbourhood names for free, while a scoreboard shows the results of two Jordan-sponsored local high school basketball teams.

It's upstairs in Centre 23, however, where Jordan's vision for Toronto can be seen. This is a state-of-the-art workout facility where local athletes can train day and night or attend sessions led by Jordan Brand trainers. In a nod to the brand heritage, there are sessions at 7am, the time that Jordan himself started training to push himself to be the best.

PREVIOUS SPREAD In order to connect with its target audience, Jordan Store is located in Yonge and Dundas, the area at the heart of Toronto's street life.

ABOVE The store has three levels: a kid's area in the basement, a retail area on the ground floor, and a gym on the upper floor that is open to local athletes day and night.

BESIDES A SUCCESSFUL RETAIL LOCATION,
NIKE WANTED TO ESTABLISH A THRIVING HUB
FOR THE CITY'S BASKETBALL COMMUNITY

Alberto Caiola

HARBOOK

Dirk Weiblen

In an era of gadgets and screens, ALBERTO CAIOLA's bookstore/ furniture showroom celebrates the luxury of the printed page

HANGZHOU — This Chinese city has been home to writers, philosophers and poets of legend, but Harbook shoulders its heritage in a progressive spirit, mixing lifestyle elements into its retail space to draw in a new generation of city-dwellers. The 600-m² bookstore, café, and contemporary Scandinavian furniture showroom, is a new model that blends tradition with aspiration.

Like a landscape in a Salvador Dalí painting, the space abstracts an urban environment — thick arches, columns, and indoor skies — a provocation to the imagination. Extending across an otherwise open-plan space, a series of thick arches evoke classical Italian porticos, which are associated with socialising, cultural exchange, shopping and dining across eras and cultures. To emphasise this cityscape, stand-alone geometric displays embellish the space like abstract sculptures and the luminous ceiling is gridded with Barrisol. The colour scheme — dusty pink, timeworn industrial concrete, silver and black — and an unconventional mash-up of materials co-exist with more classical elements. Nearby, a custom staircase ascends to a raised café area floored with locally sourced grey brick (a nod to the Chinese context in an otherwise culturally neutral environment). Overhead, an LED light installation serves as both a dramatic centrepiece and a metaphor for the enlightenment contained in books — as opposed to the ubiquitous backlit screen.

A SERIES OF THICK ARCHES EVOKE CLASSICAL ITALIAN PORTICOS, WHICH ARE ASSOCIATED WITH SOCIALISING, CULTURAL EXCHANGE, SHOPPING AND DINING

PREVIOUS SPREAD The shop resembles an abstracted Dalí landscape (before it melts), and is meant to accommodate a mixture of products.

ABOVE Postmodern geometric stand-alone displays create landmarks in the surreal landscape.

Barde + vanVoltt
SNEAKER DISTRICT

Thomas de Bruyne

BARDE + VANVOLTT designs an art gallery-like meeting point for a new generation of sneaker aficionados

ABOVE A steel powder-coated pink tunnel with illuminated by LED strips guides customers through the store, connecting the entrance with the back.

RIGHT The store front's flexible displays consist of concrete podiums topped with marmoreal — a hint to Nike's Elephant Print — as well as metal rod mesh and mirrored plinths. A vertical garden forms the backdrop to this space, which is lit by factory skylights.

ANTWERP — Amsterdam-based studio Barde + vanVoltt envisioned the 200-m² flagship for Sneaker District as a gathering place for the hardcore sneaker-head. The store foregrounds skate culture's evolving fashion agenda 'where sneakers are replacing Louboutins', as the team puts it.

Designed for one of the biggest online retailers in the Benelux, the main goal of the brand's second physical store isn't to increase sales (although iPads in a custom oak cabinet allow customers to check and order stock online). Instead, the client wanted to provide a space for visitors to enjoy a shared culture, with sneakers at the centre. It is only fitting, then, that the store's front can be easily converted to an open space for events or brand collaborations. It features concealed LED lighting for a nightclubbing experience, as well as a hang-out nook that can be turned into a stage for musicians after office hours.

'In search for materials we were inspired by sneaker design, the neighbourhood and how sneakers are made,' the designers say. A charcoal grey facade and a storefront filled with an antique pink cabinet reference the surrounding Kloosterstraat antiques district. What is more, the bright pink mesh displays and cabinets hints at the mesh used for the toes of sneakers.

Batek Architekten
ZALANDO BEAUTY STATION

BATEK ARCHITEKTEN puts forward a social media-worthy, customisable environment

BERLIN — Out of a dark space cluttered with old shop fixtures, shelves and a low ceiling, local studio Batek Architekten excavated a luminous, convertible space that can become many things to many people: a backdrop for beauty services and product presentations, video shoots and pop-up events. Minimalist, even austere in ways, it feels gossamer with light, finely textured and richly functional.

To create this 'insta-worthy' and easily customisable 130-m^2 space, the team chose a bright colour palette of cream, light beige, grey, nude and natural shades, which blend airily with the cement-bonded industrial flooring and columns and the daylight-reproducing high colour-index lighting. This gives the space the feeling of a gallery, ideal for myriad showcases.

Three ovoid floor-to-ceiling shelves made of stainless steel offer maximum flexibility and neutrality of look. These can pivot to divide the floor in two, creating a secluded rear area, or open the space up entirely. On their reverse sides, they are fitted with full-length mirrors that help to visually enlarge the space. A sleek solid concrete wash basin anchors the retail area at the front, while a 4-m-long stainless steel counter equipped with retractable mirrors draws the eye to the rear where a movable curtain made from a lightweight textile, offers privacy.

RIGHT The whitewashed, smooth neutrality of the renovated surfaces stand in contrast to the cement-bonded industrial flooring and columns.

FOLLOWING SPREAD Pivoting stainless steel shelving can divide the room in two or open up its sightlines.

Marcus Wend

CBA Clemens Bachmann Architekten
ENOTHEK BRIENNER STRASSE

Flexibility is key in CBA's concept for a wine shop that transforms from day to night

MUNICH — Converting an office into a retail environment can be challenging, especially when the new function has to serve multiple purposes. Enotheque Brienner Strasse is a bistro and wine shop during the day but, due in part to its location near the city's museum quarter, turns into an event space in the evening. Therefore, its interior needed to be able to switch functions with a minimum of fuss while retaining an overall theme.

Taking care of the functional requirements was straightforward for CBA: movable gold-lacquered steel shelves and wooden tables were installed, enabling the room to be swiftly reorganised and restructured for a variety of functions and group sizes. Wood, in the form of oak panels, is also used for the serving and sales counter that is the centre of attention whether it's day or night. Its protruding blocks add depth and an element of visual interest that entices visitors to the food and drink on display here. Burgundy curtains are a further reminder that this is a world of wine, whose ruler is paid tribute to on the ceiling. This is filled by a 100-m² print of Arianna, Venere e Bacco by Il Tintoretto, a classical painting from 1576 that depicts Bacchus, the Roman God of Wine.

RIGHT Wine is sold and tasted on tables that sit between burgundy carpets on the floor and a giant image of Bacchus on the ceiling.

FOLLOWING SPREAD Movable shelving units and tables enable the interior to switch quickly between its two roles: a shop during the day and events venue at night.

Curiosity
GINZA SIX

Satoshi Shigeta

CURIOSITY brings a shopping complex down to human scale through a crafted, angled layout

TOKYO — Ginza Six, the largest shopping complex in Tokyo's most famous upmarket shopping district, would be able to offer its customers every kind of product and experience they could conceivably desire. Yet its owners still had one overwhelming concern: how can we encourage customers to explore the entire space and stay for as long as possible? Local studio Curiosity decided the answer would be to make it welcoming as well as inspiring.

To lend the gigantic space a human aspect, each of the 241 stores has been given a different shape and its own identity. The corridor layout has also been angled to provide a fresh perspective around every corner, so that visitors should feel like they are wandering around a traditional Ginza alley, not a mall.

The central atrium is the beating heart of the mall, a space that strikes a balance between Japanese tradition and futuristic architecture. Elevators and floors run into each other to create a dynamic atmosphere of constant movement that drives customers through the space. A further invitation to explore is laid out in the sightlines that offer a clear view of every floor and area from the atrium. As a final touch, Curiosity worked closely with Japanese artisans and artists to bring a human touch to the interior, as exemplified by the columnar lighting installation that stands at the entrance, evoking the traditional Andon.

LEFT Ginza Six's corridor layout has short lines of sight so that visitors feel there is something new to discover around every corner.

ABOVE Icons and graphical elements have been used throughout the shopping complex to ensure easy navigation. For example, the elevator hall is represented by angled lines.

FOLLOWING SPREAD The Asanoha (hemp leaf) pattern on the ceiling creates a warm and inviting atmosphere that is unique to Ginza Six.

THE CENTRAL ATRIUM STRIKES A BALANCE BETWEEN JAPANESE TRADITION AND FUTURISTIC ARCHITECTURE

David Chipperfield Architects Milan
SSENSE MONTREAL

DAVID CHIPPERFIELD creates an orthogonally, industrially, austerely elegant space that can change as fast as fashion

ABOVE The historical stone and brick facades of a mid-19th century edifice were preserved along with their elegant columns and arched windows. Crowning the building, on the top floor, is a bookstore and café brightly lit by tube lights and a large skylight.

FOLLOWING SPREAD LEFT A five-floor interior made of black sandblasted concrete, cast in-situ — a nod to the area's concrete architecture — was inserted into the existing structure, increasing the historical building's stability, minimising the load-bearing interior architectural elements and leaving retail floors relatively uncluttered.

FOLLOWING SPREAD RIGHT Visually and physically lightweight displays hang from steel cables that can be clipped into a ubiquitous grid of holes in the concrete, emphasising the garments and accessories instead of the shelving.

MONTREAL — Ssense is a Canadian online fashion platform with a global presence. The harbinger of a series of brick-and-mortar locations to come, David Chipperfield Architects Milan's concept is ponderously corporeal, in counterpoint to the brand's successful virtual identity, eminently adaptable and high-tech.

The architects preserved the heritage brick and stone shell of a derelict mid-19th century building on the Rue Saint-Sulpice in Montreal's old town. Inside, they tucked five stacked boxes of black sandblasted concrete, cast in-situ (with walls and ceilings made from gleaming steel or weatherproof grating). The interiors are regulated throughout by a grid that maps down to details, from architecture to fixtures and display furniture. A grid of holes in the concrete carries wiring for a flexible lighting system and clips to hold high-tension steel cables. These can be extended from floor-to-ceiling or even wall-to-wall to carry bespoke rails, shelving and display cases. These featherweight fixtures can be easily installed and broken down, creating 'a sense of transience, in line with the e-commerce concept of rapid change and evolving needs,' the team says.

The store allows the brand to host events on the lower two floors. A double-height entrance lobby can be found on the ground floor and a glazed rooftop café on the top floor. What is more, the online and physical stores work in tandem, phygitally: orders made in the web shop can be delivered to the store for shoppers to try on.

Simon Menges

LIGHTWEIGHT DISPLAY FURNITURE CREATES 'A SENSE OF
TRANSIENCE, IN LINE WITH THE E-COMMERCE CONCEPT
OF RAPID CHANGE AND EVOLVING NEEDS'

DAVID CHIPPERFIELD ARCHITECTS MILAN

SSENSE MONTREAL

DFROST Retail Identity
ESSENCE MAKER SHOP

Ulrich Schaarschmidt

ABOVE The lounge offers a respite from cosmetics creation and is the centre point for online and offline networking.

RIGHT Inspirational messages are spread throughout the pop-up store to lead visitors to mini factories where they can make their own cosmetics.

The ultimate selfie space by DFROST inspires visitors to truly engage with a pop-up shop

BERLIN — To celebrate its 15th anniversary European cosmetics brand cosnova launched essence Maker Shop, an interactive pop-up store where young customers could create their own cosmetic products and take them home in personalised packaging just a few minutes later. The concept was sure to be a hit, but DFROST was charged with ensuring that visitors would fully engage with the space and share the results with their social networks.

With this in mind, most of the walls were left untouched to create a factory atmosphere that balanced a hands-on, industrial edge with fun, playful graphics. Neon signs and brightly illustrated inspirational texts provided encouragement to get involved in the colourful customisation stations. That was not, however, the illustrations' only goal — these were also designed to form the perfect selfie background, as everything else in the temporary space. Inside a colourful lounge, for instance, a large mirror allows customers to check out their new look, take a photo and connect with other visitors. Digital networking is taken to another level in the Instagram corner, where selfies could be uploaded online and preserved for posterity by being printed out with a special hashtag printer designed by DFROST.

ADD
olour
O YOUR
ife

FUN

LOVE

3

I'M
MATT

JSPR
FOUR BY AZZURO

Courtesy of JSPR

JSPR brings every young man's dream to life with the ultimate man cave

AMSTERDAM — In 2012, JSPR was commissioned to design and build Four, a high-end fashion store for men in the Dutch capital. Six years later, the brand moved around the corner, and JSPR was once again asked for a concept. This time, however, store owner Edward De Jonge's vision was a bigger, more impressive space focused on a particular target group: young men with taste. According to the studio founder and head designer Jasper van Grootel, there was only one way to reach this hard to impress demographic: creating the ultimate man cave. 'It has everything that young men with style like: superb sound, art, drinks, fire and very cool fashion,' he says.

A masculine tone is set with concrete floors, grey walls and tempered steel fixtures, which are the only permanent things in a space that constantly changes. Clothing racks and even the changing rooms are moveable, allowing the interior to transform for any event or arrangement. There's one island of relative stability in this sea of change, a convertible centrepiece that during the day serves as a pay desk, store cupboard, packaging area and coffee corner. During the night, however, it has already been used as a DJ booth. Artistic zones spread throughout the store host work from Dutch artists and designers that are updated regularly to stop anyone from getting bored. Completing the concept, you'll find a functioning fireplace with two sofas in front of it, right in the middle of the store.

PREVIOUS SPREAD LEFT Clothing racks and display cases are attached to wall-mounted swing-arms that enable the space to be easily reconfigured.

ABOVE The counter of this lifestyle store can be converted into a DJ booth or bar, as the occasion demands.

A CONVERTIBLE CENTREPIECE
SERVES AS PAY DESK, STORE
CUPBOARD, PACKAGING AREA
AND COFFEE CORNER

Kapsimalis Architects
THE OPEN MARKET IN OIA

Giorgos Sfakianakis

KAPSIMALIS ARCHITECTS uses an island's white architecture as inspiration to create a blank canvas for market displays

SANTORINI — This 450-m² open market, selling souvenirs, design objects and Greek craft items, takes its cues from its location at the heart of the traditional island village of Oia.

The client asked the architects to create 10 small pavilions that resemble the island's own white architecture. Built in various geometric forms, they each display a different type of product or simply conceal storage. On the site, the pre-existing memorial structure and vaulted ceiling structure were preserved as-is. The architects constructed a thick, white wall in front of the old buildings, creating two entrances and a cash till. Two of the units at the entrance serve as storefronts while the others are arranged around the perimeter. They all serve as a blank canvas that foregrounds the products conspicuously.

A long wooden table at centre displays traditional products and herbs under a canopy that resembles old fishing nets. They provide shade and add to the colour palette, helping the fresh-faced structures sit easily beside the historical ones. Altogether, despite its newness and diverse, crisp geometries, which contrast with the peeling texture and sepia tone of the older structures, the new market fits into the site, and the village, almost naturally.

LEFT The variously shaped voids in the pavilions frame the land and seascape around them and cast sculptural shadows.

FOLLOWING SPREAD The open market combines existing historical structures with 10 new geometric pavilions that have different shapes because they display different items. Some have interior spaces that can be entered while others 'host' products or hide storage.

DESPITE ITS CRISP GEOMETRY AND TEXTURE, THE
NEW MARKET FITS ORGANICALLY INTO THE VILLAGE

Knoblauch
SPORT FÖRG

A sports store moves with the times thanks to a fluid concept by KNOBLAUCH

FRIEDBERG — Despite its name, Sport Förg's owners didn't want it to look like a normal sports store. Instead, designers Knoblauch imbued the interior with the soul of sport: movement. The German studio's dynamic design aims to prove that action speaks louder than words. A challenge is issued on the storefront — 'If you have the will, we have what it takes' — an invitation to purchase equipment and put it to use immediately in a fully working 50-m² gym.

    If that all sounds a bit serious, kids of any age can take a ride on the slide on the 11-m-wide staircase in the centre of the store. The idea of movement is further supported by an angular graphic system that breaks up panels to form lines that surge across the store and establish a dynamic environment. Instead of the photography of famous athletes that usually dominates sport stores, product areas are signalled by giant human silhouettes that indicate athletic movement without relating to a specific sport. This ambiguity allows products to be positioned in every area depending on the season. For further flexibility, category signs are attached to separate shelves so that they can be easily moved together with the respective products.

Jens Pfisterer

LEFT Maritime pine is used in the central staircase and product displays to add a homely touch to the store.

BELOW Walls made of black MDF and an anthracite shop fitting system were chosen to highlight the colourful products.

Kokaistudios
NINGBO ALT-LIFE

A bookstore is a library is an events space is a café, thanks to KOKAISTUDIOS' modular zoning

NINGBO — Books are serious business in Ningbo, a town in East China that hosts the oldest library in Asia. Kokaistudios was charged with writing the next chapter in this illustrious literary history by creating a bookstore that would be as much a cultural as a commercial destination. As well as spaces to browse books, read and study, the design had to incorporate an auditorium and a variety of refreshment stands. To complicate matters even further, third-party tenants would operate some of these facilities, so the design would have to include multiple programmes and brand identities while remaining consistent and inviting.

To unite all these elements, the Shanghai-based studio channelled the spirit of Michelangelo Pistoletto's 1960s labyrinthine playgrounds to install a modular system of transparent standing shelves and corrugated cardboard counters. These are initially connected via a spiralling bookshelf that runs from the entrance, through the mezzanine and all the way down the main floor below. In doing so, the seeds of movement and discovery are planted in visitors' minds. To allow visitors to explore the store at their own pace, communal areas alternate with alcoves for contemplation and quiet. By playing with height (social zones are double the height of solitary areas), the design encourages people to move towards the action or take refuge in a quieter place, depending on their mood.

PREVIOUS SPREAD Translucent acrylic panels integrated in the white bookshelf modules allow daylight to shine through the glass pavilion and flood the interior.

BELOW The client's goal for the bookstore was to create 'a place for people to linger and spend time in', with entertainment options including a variety of refreshment areas and a 90-seat event space.

KOKAISTUDIOS' DESIGN CHANNELS THE SPIRIT OF MICHELANGELO PISTOLETTO'S LABYRINTHINE PLAYGROUNDS

COOKING
STAGE

Landini Associates
THE KITCHENS

Ross Honeysett

LEFT Industrial elements, including wire fencing, concrete columns and exposed piping, establish a food factory feel.

ABOVE The concept was inspired by European food markets and Landini Associates' takeaways from its portfolio of food projects.

FOLLOWING SPREAD LEFT The designers handled every part of the concept behind The Kitchens including brand strategy, programme and product proposals, master planning, interior and identity design, way-finding and packaging.

FOLLOWING SPREAD RIGHT Culinary delicacies are made in front of customers who can see the skill involved before purchasing the product.

A food factory on an industrial scale is given a human heartbeat by LANDINI ASSOCIATES

ROBINA — Some briefs are simple, some are less so. For this project, Landini Associates was given a 13,000-m² building in which to reinvent food retailing in Australia. In response, the Australian design firm created a cultural destination that brings the food production chain to life in all its dramatic glory in The Kitchens: a two-storey food hall, food court and food factory, where visitors can see food being made, eat it and buy it to take home.

The client was after a retail revolution, which the project achieved by bringing together food retailers and manufacturers under one roof for the first time in Queensland. The team tackled every part of the concept, from strategy to signage. 'The intention was to create a neutral backdrop to all the multi-sensory activity that is simple, urban yet classic, allowing the food and the people making and enjoying it, to be the heroes,' the designers explain.

Metal and glass are the two main materials used throughout the interior: the first establishes the atmosphere of a professional kitchen, while the second provides transparency between retailers and customers. Being able to see what is being made (and where the ingredients come from) raises a visit to The Kitchens into a genuine culinary experience. Given the venue's size, there's always something new to discover on repeat visits.

COOKING
SCHOOL

WAY OUT   TOILETS

COOKING
STAGE

A CULTURAL DESTINATION BRINGS THE FOOD
PRODUCTION CHAIN TO LIFE IN ALL ITS GLORY

Neri&Hu Design and Research Office
LITTLE B

COLOUR, SHAPES AND LIGHTING BLUR BOUNDARIES AND ACTIVATE THE SPACE

NERI&HU elevates the convenience store concept, making it a beacon of city life

SHANGHAI — Considering the convenience store as an urban beacon and a sanctuary, Neri&Hu designed this 60-m^2 retail shop and gallery for popular lifestyle brand The Beast in Xintiandi, the commercial centre of the city. An elevation of the typical corner shop concept, Little B sells light food and drink, personal care items, and basic home accessories meticulously curated from the products of high-end local and international brands and aimed at the cosmopolitan Chinese urbanite.

The architects modelled the storefront on traditional Shanghainese Shikumen lane houses, respecting existing design elements, while tapping fresh details and materials, including bespoke neon signs. Customers enter an exhibition space hosting changing art installations or marquee brand showcases and pop-up events before passing onto the retail floor.

On the retail floor, custom stainless steel display fixtures wrap the entire perimeter. By layering different materials like copper, marble and concrete with variously finished versions of stainless steel — brushed, polished, perforated and embossed — the designers give a usually cold material new warmth. Dynamic product packaging, colour schemes and shapes bring the space to life and interact with lighting given off by the custom signage, blurring boundaries and activating the space through reflections. 'While fulfilling its inherent demand for efficiency and functionality,' the studio says, 'every designed element, detail and material choice embodies the desire for a bit of humanity to grasp onto.'

PREVIOUS SPREAD Based on local vernacular architecture while adding new materials and custom signage by Neri&Hu, the facade extends an existing grey aggregate concrete into a canopy and base for the window display.

LEFT AND ABOVE The shop's function, look and feel springboard off the perfunctory character of the modern convenience store, the spontaneity and ephemerality of street culture and pop-ups 'while staying true to a timeless aesthetic that doesn't rely on instant gratification.'

Nike Design
NIKE HOUSE OF INNOVATION 000

NIKE DESIGN wills costumers into activity through a movement-shaped design

NEW YORK — One of Nike's central tenets is that everyone is an athlete, and everything in this flagship, aka Nike House of Innovation 000, is geared towards awakening, if not improving, the sportsperson that lies within us all.

The dynamism bursting out of the six-floor store is signalled by the triangle-shaped chunk taken out of the first level, marking the entrance. A design gesture which is right on brand and on message: the ceiling is angled at 23.5 degrees, the same angle as the iconic Nike Swoosh, at the same time, it is intended as a visual reference to a sprinter launching from the starting blocks. Continuing this urge for activity, the store exterior itself seems to move, thanks to the slumped and carved glass that reflects the cars flying by at the busy intersection outside, while creating its own illusion of movement as light bounces off it day and night.

Inside, every floor has a different look and feel matched to each product area, a constant transition that aims to express the fluidity of sport. As the design team exemplifies, 'the first floor's Nike Arena is dramatic and dark, focusing on the brand's innovation stories that are showcased in the space. The second-floor Women's and Young Athlete space is light and bright to experience the best of the innovative products.' In line with the innovation enshrined in the store's name, it's not just the design of each floor that changes. The tiles in the Nike Arena can be rearranged into new spaces, making it a store that really is on the move.

SPATIAL AND MATERIAL TRANSITIONS AIM TO EXPRESS THE FLUIDITY OF SPORT

PREVIOUS SPREAD LEFT The store's fourth floor hosts the Nike Sneaker Lab, the biggest Nike footwear floor in the world.

PREVIOUS SPREAD RIGHT Nike's design team developed the initial vision, then teamed up for concept development with Rockwell Group and Mode Lab, using the brand's bank of athlete data and computational design to create a feeling of lightweight speed and motion in the store.

LEFT TOP The store's fourth floor hosts the Nike Sneaker Lab, the biggest Nike footwear floor in the world.

Party/Space/Design
CHOCOLATE FACTORY

Chocolate says
"I'm sorry" & "Thank you"
so much better than words.

ABOVE After researching regional colonial architecture, which emphasised mass and void, the designers created an open space, making a luxury of its bright airy void filled with natural light by a large skylight.

PARTY/SPACE/DESIGN builds a chocolate palace that is a destination inspired by the history of its location

HUA HIN — The province of Hua Hin has escaped some of the development that has consumed other Thai resorts, but it is still very much a destination. Party/Space/Design's client asked the team to make this chocolate-centric café and shop a destination too.

After researching the history of the Hua Hin region, including its vernacular and sea-side colonial architecture — the Klai Kangwon Palace, Hua Hin train station and Maruekhathaiyawan Palace, to name a few examples — the designers worked to 'unfold the structure' of these buildings and translate them into a new architecture that contains the old. In particular, the concept of designing around mass and void, set them to work to create a generous open space at the heart of the restaurant. On one side of the building's gabled roof, a large skylight lets natural light flow into the window-wrapped kitchen, visible from the retail floor, where the chocolate is made.

The creamy white and blond wood of surfaces and bronze detailing of ductwork and pendant lamps frame an airy, bright space. Sapphire-hued upholstery recalls Benjarong, the painted Royal Porcelain of Thailand, while a graphical toile wallpaper references a bygone imperial era. Through interior decor and reference to national visual arts and culture, the store narrates 'the long legend' of Hua Hin.

Schmidhuber
SIEMENS SHOWROOM

Jörg Hempel

ABOVE Covering an area of almost 750-m² spread over two floors, the showroom is Siemens' largest brand store in Europe.

Seeing is believing in a retail concept by SCHMIDHUBER that showcases products in real-life situations

AMSTERDAM — When is a showroom not a showroom? When it's a home. Schmidhuber was asked to create a space that would bring Siemen's 'Be Connected. Everywhere' message to life, a brief that the German design studio took almost literally by placing the brand's products into real-life situations.

The design concept is based on the insight that brand experience is decisive for a customer's purchase decision. And if the products will be used at home, then what better way to show them off than in a domestic situation? Every item is showcased in one of three themed presentation areas: living room, kitchen and utility room. All of these have been realistically set up to ensure that visitors don't feel that they are in a showroom, but a show home.

Nonetheless, the experience is more than just aesthetic. All the devices are connected and controlled via an app, which visitors can use to judge the benefits of this system for themselves. This idea of seamless living is supported in the store design by visual axes that ensure the customer journey is as smooth and enjoyable as the technology. 'This way', the designers conclude, 'visitors immediately become part of the Siemens ecosystem that connects all areas of life.'

Studio Amber
WARRECORDS

STUDIO AMBER creates a space that brings people together, just like the music sold there

ANTWERP — This 40-m² record store is a hang-out predicated on music. Beat connoisseurs come to listen to or stock up on vinyl, watch live DJ's and bands, or view an art exhibit over a Belgian beer with buddies. The shop is occupied morning, noon and night because it hosts daytime and morning-after DJ sessions. It is a space that, at any hour, is designed to connect people to and through music.

In a nod to the underground music scene, local Studio Amber used industrial materials, including perforated steel, concrete and unfinished brick walls. As visitors enter the small space, it feels transparent and open although they must circumnavigate a long display running down the centre of the room. This piece of furniture determines a circulation pattern that ensures everyone casts an eye over the merchandise first thing.

Functional square perforated steel furniture, including displays and a DJ booth, is both flexible and demountable within a given gridded framework. To determine the dimensions of this grid, designer Amber Feijen took cues from the square of a vinyl cover, which measures 30 × 30 cm and, as one of the most fundamental geometric shapes, is easy on the eye, suggesting both stability and forthrightness.

LEFT References to the underground music scene are palpable in this record store and event space.

BELOW The custom furniture and displays, including the DJ booth were built around a grid based on the dimensions of a record album cover.

FOLLOWING SPREAD The designer used industrial materials like perforated steel and raw brick. The purpose-made central display means visitors see much of the merchandise just to enter the store

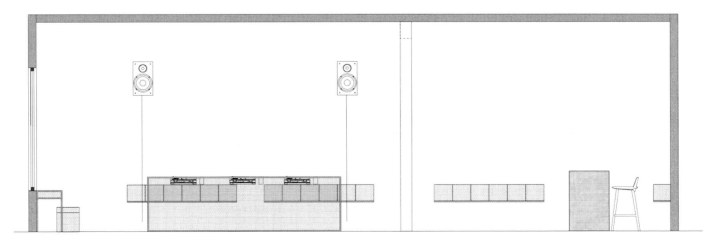

Studio DLF
SLFT

Spy mirrors and scan stations play into STUDIO DLF's futuristic design

CONSTANCE — This sleek shop manifests Studio DLF's belief that 'design is the aesthetic interpretation of logic.' A 150-m², two-floor flagship for a multi-brand store, it displays and sells trainers and other streetwear with the use of discoverable spy mirrors and scan stations. The designer Daniele Luciano Ferrazzano combined user-friendly technologies with futuristic-looking materials — white Italian terrazzo and smoked mirrors, acrylic double-wall sheets and epoxy resin floors — to choreograph a fresh shopping experience.

For big brands like Nike or Adidas, select products can be displayed on special merchandising walls behind black glass 'spy mirrors'. When spots light the products from inside, they render the mirror transparent, making the products look like hidden holograms. The same method allows customers to 'discover' RFID scan station screens behind the spy mirrors, where they can watch a 360-degree product video and access data on stocking and price. Special edition or rare footwear is displayed on illuminated semi-transparent acrylic walls, or 'power walls'.

By establishing a dominant grid, as the need arises, displays can be easily expanded with shelves, tablets or rails without interrupting the shop's clean lines and user-friendliness. Playful details like a pulsing light installation near the entrance and a locker room-inspired point of sale also embellish that basic grid without disturbing the store's sleek futuristic look.

TOP RIGHT Scan stations are screens integrated into tables and walls behind black 'spy mirror' glass that are only visible when illuminated from within. Data on look, product availability and price, as well as 360-degree videos, are viewable here.

BOTTOM RIGHT The walls contain a fixed grid to which additional shoe-presenter-sticks, shelves, tablets or garment rails can be added, as the need arises.

FOLLOWING SPREAD The ground floor shoe wall is made of smoked glass. DLF translated the look of sneakers into monolithic display furniture and seating cubes, then used high-tech sneaker fabric to upholster the seats.

STUDIO ROY DE SCHEEMAKER's timeless cosmopolitan design draws on the personality of the brand it houses

ROTTERDAM — Studio Roy de Scheemaker has been designing stores for Skins Cosmetics a global retailer in niche, high-end fragance, skincare, make-up and lifestyle products, around the globe for a decade. Developed in collaboration with Tchai and De Pander, 300-m² location offers the brand's entire library of scents while also allowing shoppers to experience products directly in the second-floor City Spa.

In order to amplify the brightness, cleanliness and transparency of the space, de Scheemaker backlit the walls from floor-to-ceiling. The airbrushed midnight blue ceiling serves as a neutral background for the bespoke, jewelry-like lighting object made up of vertically suspended acrylic sheets that bridge the store's two rooms. A modest concrete floor by Holland Flooring International was veined with polished brass according to the principles of the Japanese kintsugi philosophy, which preserves flaws in old ceramics by filling them with a precious metal.

Every Skins location, within the global concept, is unique in some way, a uniqueness expressed through materials and details. Here, the materials of high and low culture collide — concrete with polished brass and red copper countertops, acrylic and precious wood with aged metals — in a way that de the designer feels is characteristic of Rotterdam.

Studio Roy de Scheemaker
SKINS COSMETICS

Studio XAG
NAPAPIJRI

STUDIO XAG cuts through the high street cacophony to turn a community focused pop-up into a permanent retail jungle

LONDON — Studio XAG was tasked with envisioning the first physical UK retail location of this Italian premium casual wear brand on a crowded high street in Shoreditch. Initially, the project began as a temporary pop-up in an 85-m² corner building that took its visual cues from Napapijri's SS18 Out of Nowhere campaign, which was set in a deserted wilderness.

To mark the brand's arrival with impact, the facade is drenched in an eye-catching orange hue and features a supersized logo wrapping the storefront. Inside, an abstracted desert installation was made eminently adaptable and attractive whilst conspicuously offering no product for sale. The retailer focused instead on hosting cultural experiences — partnering with 28 local 'heroes' of alternative culture, from zine publishers and DJ's to artists — to raise brand awareness. By mounting screens, creating a gallery and staging area and crafting portable furniture, the team made the store not just reconfigurable, but repurposable.

Success eventually transformed the space into a semi-permanent concept shop focused on digital innovation, product narratives, brand experience and engagement. The anchor of the newly developed interior is a sculptural jungle that is reflected in mirrors lining the walls of the store: enlarging the space visually, pulling visitors into Napapijri's world.

LEFT Studio XAG introduced Napapijri to London with a temporary installation that engulfed the facade in fluorescent orange, utilising billboards and an oversized logo to cut through the noise of a saturated high street.

BELOW A monolithic mirror installation emerges from earth-like terrain, flanked by high impact lightboxes which display brand content.

FOLLOWING SPREAD The designers modelled the new space on the brand's famous rainforest jacket, creating a lush interior jungle.

Melvyn Vincent Photography

UNStudio
LANE 189

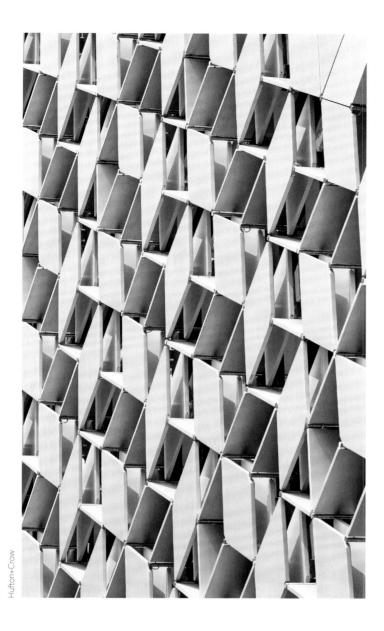

Hutton+Crow

The only way is up in a mall re-arranged into a vertical city by UNSTUDIO

SHANGHAI — Lane 189 is a shopping centre that enriches its retail appeal with restaurant and office spaces. In order to lure in the city's young professionals, Amsterdam-based architects UNStudio turned tradition on its head by founding a vertical city that reflects the neighbourhood's existing identity while standing out boldly with a futuristic facade.

'The design incorporates elements of "old Shanghai" through geometry, pattern and materialisation and combines these with a contemporary urban experience, thereby creating a destination with a distinctly Shanghai feel,' explain the designers. City and mall are connected by double-height openings in the facade. Depending on the level, what UNStudio calls 'urban eyes' can act as display platforms for people looking in, or balconies that look out over the surroundings, including nearby Chang Shou Park.

Once inside, visitors are guided towards a slow or fast shopping experience. Centrally located escalators allow customers to circulate casually between each level, while anyone in a hurry can hop on the elevators which are easy to spot thanks to the transparent lift cabins. These are hosted in the central core of Lane 189, a void that offers a complete view of the vertical city from top to bottom, including a series of rounded plateaus. Each plateau has an individual theme: a market plaza and food court can be found on the lower level, while the first and second level plateaus hold an art street and grand balcony.

LEFT A transition from bigger to smaller facade components regulates the exposure of the inside to the outside, allowing the facade to become an active layer that can be programmed as display windows, vista points or balconies.

ABOVE Based on a hexagonal grid, the facade components follow the articulated geometry of the building and provide constantly changing perspectives.

FOLLOWING SPREAD All the levels of the 'vertical city' are visible from the central void at the heart of Lane 189, which offers a clear view from the second basement level right up to an art installation in the skylight.

A VOID OFFERS A COMPLETE VIEW OF
THE VERTICAL CITY FROM TOP TO BOTTOM

UNStudio
TERMINAL 2 LANDMARK SPACE

UNSTUDIO creates an oasis of calm in the heart of a major airport

INCHEON — Airports are busy places at the quietest of times and Incheon Airport is the largest airport in South Korea. Amidst the relentless footfall in its second terminal, UNStudio was asked to create 'a microclimate where passengers can eat, drink and find a moment of relaxation along their journey.'

This oasis is the Landmark Space, whose presence, just like in the desert, is signalled by a mass of greenery arising from barren surroundings. Passengers who have become inured to the terminal's sterile white lines and marble floors are greeted by the welcoming sight of two wooden pavilions with roofs overflowing with climbing plants. Wood was chosen to offer a warm welcome to travellers as well as for its therapeutic benefits. According to UNStudio, 'The health and wellbeing of the traveller is improved through the introduction of natural materials such as wood, water and greenery.'

Further food for the soul is provided in the lounge and seating area that connects the two pavilions. The design of the built-in furniture in this area facilitates every kind of activity, from individual areas for work or quiet contemplation to shared spaces for socializing. Whatever a passenger wishes to do here, the Landmark Space's wooden borders are filled with more plants to ensure that every weary passenger is enclosed within its lush, tranquil embrace.

PREVIOUS SPREAD   The canopy pavilion
draws inspiration from the branching systems
inherent in leaf structures.

LEFT The light lines in the floor and canopy
act as a pathfinding element for the pavilions.

BELOW The horizontal lamellas mimic the
terminal roof, but are made of wood to im-
part a feeling of warmth.

Woods Bagot
OVER/UNDER KIOSKS

Brooke Holm

EACH KIOSK IS IMAGINED AS ONE-HALF OF A LARGE RECTANGULAR BLOCK BISECTED BY AN UNDULATING CURVE INTO TWO COMPLEMENTARY, FLOWING VOLUMES

WOODS BAGOT blends architectural folly, street furniture and waterfront sculpture

NEW YORK — Woods Bagot sculpted the two 11-m² pop-up Over/Under beverage kiosks, from 800 aluminium cylinders and steel. The shapely pair stood for a summer serving frosty Heineken beer in Manhattan's newly master planned Seaport District. Their silhouette and texture meant that the summer sun played over the wavy walls and curves of each truncated tube.

One constraint that influenced the design was a guideline limiting any new structure in the historic district to a 2D extruded profile. Each kiosk was therefore imagined as one-half of a large rectangular block bisected by an undulating line to create complementary, flowing volumes.

The hundreds of tubes constituting the facades were individually cut using a CNC 3D laser-cutter. To ensure quick assembly and disassembly, each 15 cm laser-cut aluminium cylinder had to be labelled to help the workers put them together correctly on-site.

The complementary forms of Over/Under mean that the first, which arcs overhead, forms a sheltering 'urban grotto' equipped with a squiggly wooden bench. At the same time, the second structure curves downward to the height of a bench — which also came in handy, it just so happens, as an outdoor dance floor.

PREVIOUS SPREAD The temporary Over/Under kiosks stood 3-m-high at 11-m² each and were made from 800 aluminium cylinders.

ABOVE Woods Bagot partnered with LAUFS and Kammetal to engineer and prefabricate the kiosks which were assembled in a single afternoon.

RIGHT A green acrylic skylight casts a cool light on the bar while also serving as an element of branding.

LET'S TALK ABOUT US

RETAIL SPACE AS A MIRROR OF THE BRAND

Interview
ALEX MOK AND BRIAR HICKLING

Ambrous Young

ALEX MOK and BRIAR HICKLING, co-founders of Shanghai and Hong Kong-based architecture and interior design studio Linehouse, reflect on the importance of capturing consumer's attention through unexpected, long-lasting and meaningful brand narratives.

How do you approach retail space design? We spend time researching the brand and what their ethos is, where they are from and what influences them. We always try to create a concept that comes from the brand itself.

What do you think are the main challenges of this project typology? Our designs are always about creating an interesting spatial experience and the main challenge arising from that is striking a balance between the products and the environment we are creating. Apart from that, some of the brands we work with need to consider the bigger picture of multiple store rollouts, which means a flexible, easily translatable and quickly constructible design.

How would you define a successful retail space? Right now we are seeing a new era of shops that are bold, sensational and shocking. Gentle Monster's stores are a very good example of this trend. They are impressive spaces, extremely successful in creating awareness of the brand and appealing to the new age of the influencer, but invariably date quickly and need constant updating in order to continue to be relevant. One the other hand, we can deem success in quieter, long-lasting design solutions with brands like Aesop, whose stores speak about heritage and craft.

When developing multiple designs for the same brand, how do you balance the representation of the brand through spatial design with the need for fresh concepts? I think a good example of this is, again, Aesop. Their stores always have a fresh design, yet come back to fundamental principles of context, heritage and craft. I think once you have established a brand's fundamental principles, these can be interpreted in different ways spatially to convey the same meaning.

In your opinion, how has the discipline adapted to the challenges brought about by online shopping and 'the age of the influencer?' Retail environments are more focused on creating a spatial experience rather than pushing out products to consumers. A lot of retailers now seek out an instagrammable moment, creating interactive environments that will capture people's attention and go viral.

What, in your opinion, is the main goal of retail spaces today? As interior designers our goal when it comes to creating retail spaces is to harness a physical environment which tells the story of the brand in an unexpected way, to create a retail experience which captures one's memory and engagement.

How do you envision the future of retail design? We hope the conversation about environmental mindfulness and our planet's resources will start to affect consumer behaviour and ultimately retail design on a mass level. At the moment there are still very little retailers who are making real efforts to change the way people consume.

'ONCE YOU HAVE ESTABLISHED A BRAND'S FUNDAMENTAL PRINCIPLES, THESE CAN BE INTERPRETED INTO DIFFERENT SPATIAL DESIGNS'

Archiee
EN

What goes around comes round in ARCHIEE's polished concept for a skincare treatment centre

PARIS — The Japanese word 'en' can be interpreted in three ways: as beauty, circle and connection. It's also the name of a high-end skincare company that engaged design studio Archiee to outfit its first Parisian location. The multiple meanings of the brand's name inspired a design concept that unites all the values in a vision as clear as the skin its customers leave with.

Given the store's location in an 18th-century building, the majority of the original structural elements were left in place. For example, the brickwork in the underground vault has been left untouched apart from a coat of white paint. The main design interventions are the circular partitions that create enclosed spaces for personal consultations, skin treatments and massages.

Nonetheless, it is impossible for customers to enter these directly. To do so, they must walk a winding path that the designers intend to express the value of connection. 'The method of letting visitors walk along a path to enhance his or her expectation is typical of the Japanese way of hospitality, similar to the traditional tea ritual,' the designers explain. Each of the partitions has a white interior to radiate purity, but polished brass exteriors to signify the idea of beauty while lending the space a comforting warmth.

PREVIOUS SPREAD RIGHT A central display features approximately 100 different cosmetic products, each of which is picked out by an individual spotlight.

BELOW The existing spaces of the 18th-century building were divided into four main rooms: two with stone vaulted spaces in the basement and two rooms finished with white plaster on the ground floor.

RIGHT Japanese paulownia wood used for the storage boxes under product displays offers an organic visual contrast to the exposed stonework of the underground vault.

Area-17
JACOB COHËN

Filippo Piantandida

AREA-17 designs a luxury denim boutique to age like a pair of jeans

MILAN — As befits designer jeans, this flamboyant boutique at the heart of the city's fashion district was designed to convey a sense of laid-back sophistication and uniqueness. Over 210-m^2 and two floors, Area-17 made the shop an artefact that will become more precious over time, like jeans that soften and conform to one's body the more they are worn.

The Italian studio created a tidy environment that is, nonetheless, able to stir the emotions by combining the neat geometry of the interior's linear elements and surfaces, with a strong colour palette. According to the team, the design 'deftly mixes deep blue, gold, and neutral shades of beige and browns, giving the sense of preciousness and laid-back elegance that has always been the brand's hallmark.'

Many of the interior textures and colours that enliven the shop were inspired by and are intended to highlight the products on display. For instance, the designers used Japanese Kurakabo denim for drapery and capitonné decorative panels, now a signature of all Cohën spaces. What is more, by using natural finishes in all materials, Area-17 was able to ensure that the store will age richly with the passage of time.

ABOVE A window display by JoAnn Tann Studio broadcasts the indigo, gold and beige palette inside in a scene that conveys the brand's high-end but casual character.

RIGHT The design represents the translation into interior architecture of the brand's commitment to 'elevate simplicity to perfection'.

THE SHOP IS AN ARTEFACT THAT WILL BECOME MORE PRECIOUS OVER TIME, LIKE JEANS THAT SOFTEN AND CONFORM TO ONE'S BODY THE MORE THEY ARE WORN

LEFT On the ground floor, polished industrial concrete flooring with wool area rug inserts, walls finished with lime-effect paint and bespoke brass details form the backdrop to the brand's collections.

atelier 522

ENGELHORN SPORTS

ATELIER 522 stages the perfect customer journey to a complete sporting universe

MANNHEIM — Located in the city's N5 square, Engelhorn Sports's 10,000-m^2 of retail space sprawl over seven floors. Recently, three of those floors were redesigned by atelier 522, who remapped the look and feel of the interiors, as well as the customer experience by broadening their interaction with the space and its displays in both analogue and digital ways.

Mixed materiality was core to the studio's plan: in the football and urban lifestyle departments, located at ground level, products are displayed between concrete and metal grids. The mood of the men's section — encompassing fitness, running and swimwear products — is darker, edgier and is staged amongst furniture made of concrete, maritime pine, metal and coarse rope. On the first and second floors, in the women's fitness and running departments, the staging is bright and smooth, relying on white ash, cork and light textiles to generate sensual contrasts.

What is more, the designers removed display walls and room dividers to draw in daylight. Overall, the revamped emporium offers a more accessible and welcoming athletic universe anchored by a generous living room atmosphere, intuitive points of sale, and entertaining product staging.

Brinkworth and Wilson Brothers
FIORUCCI

In this consumer's playground, BRINKWORTH AND WILSON BROTHERS broadcast the joyful spirit of a brand's mid-century retail interiors

Louise Melchior

LONDON — In 1967, Elio Fiorucci opened the doors onto his first Milanese boutique and the expressive, progressive, cheeky utopia that was to rocket the brand around the globe. To re-launch the label in Soho half a century later, two local teams of designers 'took a journey' through the vast archive of Fiorucci graphics and embarked on a collaboration that honours the past while looking to the future.

Over only two floors and 345-m², Brinkworth and Wilson Brothers created a dense scenography that includes an entirely mirrored upstairs ceiling, chrome light fixtures, chunky garment racks and pink resin flooring. To enable the space to 'evolve and adapt', the designers used a series of mobile stand-alone displays. There is a sunken lounge painted blue, Fiorucci's signature circular upholstered bed on a mosaic tiled platform and a staircase that spirals around a column of planters.

Start your shopping day in the ground floor café and end it on the quieter first floor, in the glossy black and white cocktail bar, Paninaro. The upstairs was inspired, in part, by the home of Cesar Manrique in Lanzarote. The designers described their concept as 'an oasis of tropical optimism in a sea of dark times'. It's just like old times.

LEFT The design team took a theatrical, caffeinated approach that features a sunken lounge, a cartoonish foam table, chrome garment racks and mobile displays that allow the space to be easily reconfigured.

FOLLOWING SPREAD LEFT Draped in bright blue, the VIP fitting room on the first floor features a bespoke, star-spangled carpet, contiguous hemisphere pendant lights and a glittering golden punching bag sporting the Fiorucci logo.

FOLLOWING SPREAD RIGHT The upstairs ceiling is entirely mirrored and reflects bespoke neon signs using artwork and graphics from early Fiorucci catalogues and heritage brand graphics. Display podiums are made from Corian cubes or flocked and rubberised foam blocks in various colours.

A JOURNEY THROUGH THE BRAND'S ARCHIVES
HONOURS THE PAST WHILE LOOKING TO THE FUTURE

POWERSHOP_6

LET'S TALK ABOUT US

Burdifilek

MACKAGE

An urban ski chalet-inspired design by BURDIFILEK encloses a brand's modern edge

TORONTO — It isn't only the Rocky Mountains that can be cold, shopping malls can also feel like hostile environments. Mackage, a Canadian outwear brand, is more familiar than most with extreme conditions, so it wanted to make sure its largest flagship store yet offered a warm welcome in a Toronto mall. Local studio Burdifilek raised the temperature with an urban ski chalet whose luxurious fittings reflect the craftsmanship and detailing of the brand's products.

The team's first step was to break up the cavernous space by installing a series of vignettes. These wooden installations are set at differing heights to create a series of warm, cocoon-like spaces that offer a respite from the world outside. Black walls, dark lighting and backlit images of the Rocky Mountains combine to drive visitors towards these warm refuges like skiers towards a chalet after a hard day on the pistes.

Although the liberal use of timber recalls a traditional wooden ski hut, Burdiflek elevates the tone with a Nero Marquina herringbone floor and brushed bronze lamps and fittings. Finally, large chunks of white Statuario marble serve as product displays and an impressive cash desk, while also bringing the world of ice and snow inside the store for a final touch of cool.

PREVIOUS SPREAD LEFT The interior is full of references to the Rocky Mountains, ranging from backlit images of snowy summits to an iceberg-like cash desk made of white Statuario marble.

PREVIOUS SPREAD RIGHT As shoppers step inside each vignette they enter a warm, intimate space that matches the brand's product philosophy.

RIGHT A Nero Marquina herringbone floor stands out against the wooden cabins to lend the store a luxurious allure.

A SERIES OF WARM, COCOON-LIKE SPACES
OFFER RESPITE FROM THE WORLD OUTSIDE

Christopher Ward Studio
OROVIVO 1856

CHRISTOPHER WARD STUDIO creates an enchanted forest to break the spell of stereotypical jewellery stores

BERLIN — There was no getting away from the fact that a jewellery store would have to contain a certain amount of fixtures — notably display cases — but OroVivo was keen to move away as far as possible from any industry stereotypes in its new boutique. This posed a creative challenge to Christopher Ward Studio: how to retain the original atmosphere of natural elements and maintain the setting rules, while breaking new ground. The balance between these directions was found by delving into the brand's Bavarian roots to create an enchanted forest.

Two natural elements, sky and earth, dominate: light blue and grey plastic pendants descend from the ceiling to form an illusion of a shower of rain; earthy tones are provided by wood that lends a natural foundation to the forest floor and potted plants scattered around the store add a subtle touch of green. In the middle of these two worlds hang the display cases, suspended from the ceiling on galvanized gold supports. By positioning the products at different heights, customers are invited to explore deeper into the forest, in a modern take on fairy tales that reflects OroVivo's quest to establish the 'new traditional'.

RIGHT OroVivo's logo, an owl, is a natural fit amongst the surroundings of an enchanted forest.

FOLLOWING SPREAD Galvanized gold was used for the product display supports to place the jewellery a suitably sparkling setting.

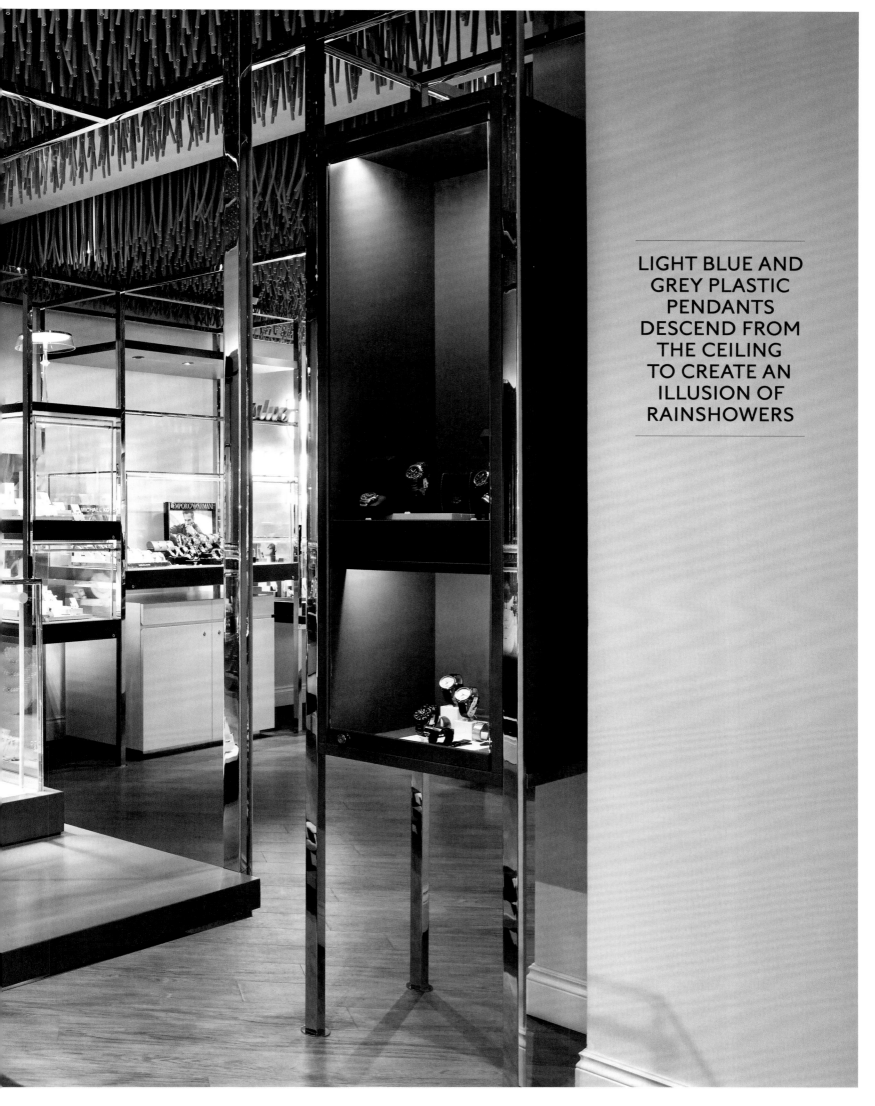

LIGHT BLUE AND
GREY PLASTIC
PENDANTS
DESCEND FROM
THE CEILING
TO CREATE AN
ILLUSION OF
RAINSHOWERS

In a concept by CISZAK DALMAS STUDIO AND MATTEO FERRARI, home is where the heart is

MADRID — Malababa is an accessories manufacturer that champions ethical production, sustainability and traditional local craftsmanship. All its products are proudly designed and made in Spain, so it was only natural that Ciszak Dalmas Studio and Matteo Ferrari would follow the same path for the brand's flagship store in the country's capital.

The two design studios teamed up with Malababa founders, Ana Carrasco and Jaime Lara, to create a space built on the brand's principles. Take the walls for example: the raw finish references the textures inherent to the products. The material is made of a mix of Galician clay, white marble powder from Almería and natural, ecological and non-toxic food thickeners. As if that didn't score enough green points, the finish also regulates air moisture and temperature and thus helps to save energy throughout the year. The tiles in the lattice structure near the entrance have an equally local provenance: they were made by artisans in Toledo with mud from quarries in Extremadura, before being baked in an ecological H2G oven fired with biomass.

But the interior has more than just green credentials. The play between light, texture, colour and shapes throughout the store creates an enticing environment that forms the perfect backdrop to Malababa's products. The effect is enhanced by the natural light that streams through the enlarged windows, bathing interior and accessories alike in a warm glow.

Asier Rua

Ciszak Dalmas Studio
and Matteo Ferrari

MALABABA

PREVIOUS SPREAD LEFT Teamwork is at the heart of this collaboration between two design studios and the Malababa founders. This is reflected in the fact that each tile in the lattice structure was placed by the hand of a team member.

PREVIOUS SPREAD RIGHT The layered leather curtain separating the store and a staff room is made by master craftsman Osvaldo Ruben Thomas with the same vegetable tanned leather used in the brand's products.

BELOW The store furniture consists of mobile modules that can be combined and rebuilt as necessary.

RIGHT Like the brand's leather products, the materials used in the store interior were chosen for their ability to gain character with age.

Claudio Pironi & Partners
BILLIONAIRE

Philipp Plein

Greek tragedy sets the scene for CLAUDIO PIRONI's homage to luxury

PARIS — Billionaire Couture offers exactly what its name promises: high-end fashion with a price tag to match. Therefore, you might not be surprised to learn that Claudio Pironi's design for the brand's Parisian flagship store aims to establish 'a place of worship dedicated to extreme luxury for international jetsetters' — but the fact that it's inspired by classic Greek tragedy might come as more of a shock.

By alternating light and dark, and packed product areas with empty space, Pironi stages 'a game of fullness and emptiness' that mirrors the descent of a hero into ruin. Fortunately, all that visitors to this store will fall into is the lap of luxury. The scenographic aspect of the iconic 1930s Parisian building, whose architecture has been restored and enhanced by Pironi's design, is emphasised by a facade made up of 8-m-high black lacquered glass windows. An opulent tone is set by an imposing Portaluppi marble staircase that connects the three floors. Its black and white veins form the colour palette extended throughout the store, where the same marble also appears in product display frames, bases and on the walls.

Lighting plays a key role in such a dark environment, which Pironi uses to maximum effect. As he puts it, 'just as in the theatre the actor is enveloped by a cone of light moving on the stage, in the same way, I duplicated the amount of illumination on the garments in order to enhance them to become the protagonists of the whole store, as in a real mise-en-scène.'

PREVIOUS SPREAD One of the walls is covered in mirrors to create what the designer describes as 'a world of sexy reflections'.

ABOVE Smoky grey mirrored walls and Portaluppi grey marble combine to amplify the store's sensory experience.

RIGHT The store's facade features huge black lacquered glass windows that rise up to 8 m.

AN OPULENT TONE IS SET BY
THE IMPOSING PORTALUPPI
MARBLE STAIRCASE THAT
CONNECTS THE THREE FLOORS

Corneille Uedingslohmann Architekten
KULT

Michael Neuhaus

CORNEILLE UEDINGSLOHMANN ARCHITEKTEN mixes laid-back materials to create an urban/ organic hybrid

OLDENBURG — Corneille Uedingslohmann's design for the 405-m² Kult multi-brand store grafts together urban, industrial, geometric elements with authentic, raw, natural materials.

At the centre of the store, a long, low plywood platform supported by white painted scaffolding displays products. Echoed in a long panel of metal mesh caging overhead, the two serve to emphasise the space's linearity, and are underscored by fluorescent lighting that points shoppers deeper into the floor.

An urban atmosphere is established by choices like tubular fluorescent light installations, scaffolding, untreated black steel, an exposed ceiling revealing technical equipment and ductwork, angular patterns and concrete-finished pendant lights. Organic elements include an existing screed floor sanded and sealed with a UV-hardening lacquer to highlight its blemishes and irregularities of colour, and metres of wooden flooring and displays. 'The use of a mixture of textures and materials divides the sales floor into smaller product areas,' the designers explain. This approach is also used to demarcate the cash desk area from the rest of the space: at the back, the shop is floored with wood planks and furnished with a concrete-slab cash desk.

LEFT A blend of cosmopolitan urban elements broadcast fresh trends in the multi-label fashion market.

ABOVE Cash desk furniture made of concrete slabs are overhung with wire and concrete dome pendants.

FOLLOWING SPREAD The central merchandising platform emphasises the depth of the store, while fluorescent tube lights arranged into arrows direct shoppers deeper into the floor.

AN URBAN ATMOSPHERE IS ESTABLISHED THROUGH
FLUORESCENT LIGHT INSTALLATIONS, SCAFFOLDING,
UNTREATED STEEL AND AN EXPOSED CEILING

Corneille Uedingslohmann Architekten
STUDIO JUSTE

CORNEILLE UEDINGSLOHMANN ARCHITEKTEN frame an eco-friendly fashion boutique with sustainable furniture and materials

COLOGNE — To create this 50-m² ecological and fair-trade fashion concept shop, local studio Corneille Uedingslohmann Architekten used simple, sustainable furniture and untreated wood surfaces. Showcasing the planet and people-friendly garments and accessories in an equally eco-friendly environment was a natural design choice.

From the street, an oversized wooden herringbone parquet floor points visitors into the shop. Inside, the walls were excavated and left unfinished, raw and peeling beneath a partially exposed ceiling where wiring and ductwork remains visible. The architects describe the contrasts created by the palette of materials as both 'optical and haptic', as it combines soft and hard, cool and warm, coarse and smooth.

A large table, fashioned from solid, indigenous wood and trimmed with powder-coated metal details, sits front and centre. To widen the narrow shop visually, a copper-tone mirrored cube was placed in the centre of the store that can double-task as a signature wall and a backdrop for the sales counter. The custom perforated wall system cladding the main wall accommodates the variable placement — and frequent reorganisation — of products of any size or type. This variety of display belies the limited depth of the shop.

Alessandra Chemollo

Curiosity
MONCLER

CURIOSITY's cool concept brings an iceberg to the desert

DUBAI — With its first boutique in the Middle East located in Dubai Mall's Fashion Avenue extension, Moncler was keen to stand out amongst its glamorous neighbours. Tokyo-based studio Curiosity decided that the best way for the Italian outerwear brand to distinguish itself was to go back to its roots and the origin of its brand name — an abbreviation of Monestier de Clermont, an Alpine town in France.

The snow and ice that dominate the winters there inspired the design concept of 'an iceberg in the desert'. This comes to life on the exterior facade with Calacatta Michelangelo marble that has been handcrafted by Italian marble masters to capture the moment an iceberg breaks. This imagery is given extra impact by the interior's dark tones. Grey Emperador marble and grey oak are used liberally to create an elegant atmosphere that illustrates snow and the mountain beneath it.

High ceilings are another Alpine allusion, with products displayed at a variety of levels to guide the visitor through the store and stop off where they please. Once customers come down from the peaks and reach the fitting rooms, they will find that these are covered with quilted white leather. However, rather than snow or ice, this is a reference to the lining of a Moncler down jacket

QUILTED WHITE
LEATHER IS A
DIRECT REFERENCE
TO THE LINING
OF A MONCLER
DOWN JACKET

Francesc Rifé

CAMPER

David Zarzoso

LEFT By inverting the traditional application of rope, steel and terracotta, the design concept gives the materials new meaning.

ABOVE The geometric simplicity of the staircase is enriched by the use of natural oak and steel details.

FOLLOWING SPREAD Fittingly for a shoe store, the terracotta tiles have been adjusted in size to that of a human footprint.

Humble materials are given a twist in FRANCESC RIFÉ's mix of tradition and innovation

FIDENZA — Francesc Rifé knew exactly what he wanted to do for this Camper store: create an environment that reflects the shoemaker's ability to balance tradition and innovation. 'We have adapted the same philosophy to this design using traditional materials such as terracotta tiles, steel, or rope, but applying them in a completely different and contemporary way,' Rifé reveals.

Terracotta is the first thing that most customers will notice — it's used for the floors and walls, but not in its famous pastel shade. Instead each tile has been dyed grey to form a neutral background that allows the shoes to stand out more dramatically. Another twist to the traditional tile format is its size, which is approximately that of a human footprint. The second design element, steel, is used for the large sales counter and staircase that dominate the store.

Large panels of grey smoked glass in the staircase provide a level of transparency, a theme which is mirrored by the ropes on the top floor. These hang in tribute to Camper's shoelaces and remain in their natural state to honour the material's purity. There's sufficient space between each rope to provide a glimpse into the storage space behind, a solution intended by the designer to connect the products and the store design.

THE SPACE REFLECTS
THE BRAND'S ABILITY TO
BALANCE TRADITION
AND INNOVATION

Ippolito Fleitz Group

HUNKE

Zooey Braun

IPPOLITO FLEITZ GROUP invests a jewellery shop and optician with a rich blend of intimacy and grandeur

LUDWIGSBURG — For a family-run optician and jeweller, Stuttgart-based identity architects Ippolito Fleitz Group consolidated the different departments into a comprehensive interior plan capable of incorporating family tradition and the building's aristocratic history. The shop has a rich sobriety and combines grand and intimate spaces. Whatever their scale, each area is wholly modern, tranquil and luxurious.

The 1400-m² sales and display areas were integrated into the listed building of former court jeweller Kiesel. Large windows look into the prestigious shop interior, so that the space itself becomes part of the window display.

The jewellery and optical departments possess a cohesive look, but each are distinguished by colours and materials — more regal and more urban, respectively — that articulate their differing product ranges. In the first, dark curtains stand behind brightly backlit white shelves recalling cosmetic tables or vanities while inconspicuous black cabinets provide copious storage. In the second, shelves of muted translucent colours identify the areas containing sunglasses and corrective eyeglasses, while scarlet shelves mark the transition to the jewellery department. Mixing new and old, muted and imposing, grandeur and the human scale, the result is a lush environment of welcoming intimacy and patrician modernity.

PREVIOUS SPREAD One goal was to create a frame for every one of the brand's extensive collection of eyewear and jewellery. Mirrors integrated into the floors and flanking display shelves give the space an almost residential feeling.

BELOW The optical department combines angles and crisp lines, bursts of savoury colour, serene lighting, softening fabrics and carpets in watercolour hues to create a feeling of calm and warmth.

RIGHT The space-generous jewellery department is draped with curtains and carpet over polished screed, marble and braided metals.

THE JEWELLERY AND OPTICAL DEPARTMENTS
POSSESS A COHESIVE LOOK, BUT EACH ARE
DISTINGUISHED BY COLOURS AND MATERIALS

POWERSHOP 6 LET'S TALK ABOUT US

Jonathan Leijonhufvud

Linehouse

HERSCHEL SUPPLY SHIBUYA

PREVIOUS SPREAD The facade features angled battens, backed with aluminium panels,
painted blue on one side and left bare on the
other so that the approach looks different
from each side.

ABOVE The second floor draws the exterior
treatment inside, using the partly painted
wood battens in vertical rows as display.

THE STORE'S
FACADE LOOKS
DIFFERENT
DEPENDING ON
THE DIRECTION OF
ONE'S APPROACH

LINEHOUSE reimagines retail space as a cabin in the city's wilderness

TOKYO — For Herschel's store in the Japanese capital, Linehouse tapped the Canadian lifestyle brand's roots in Vancouver, a city surrounded by wilderness. The designer's reinterpretation of the mountain cabin for the metropolis resulted in a neatly exploded version of its rustic inspiration: an 'urban-forest' architecture.

Linehouse stacked wood battens to mark the store's threshold. The angled battens are lightly finished on one side and painted in various tones of blue on the other. Thanks to this, the store's facade looks different depending on the direction of one's approach. On either side, more battens, stacked horizontally and cut at an angle, frame voids that serve as window display space.

Past the pivoting door, the space opens up like a clearing in a forest. From concrete floor to illuminated stretch ceiling, the walls of this indoor/outdoor room are lined with hand-etched stainless steel panels. The etching fades vertically, creating a matte surface below eye level and a mirror-polish surface above. At the back of this 'clearing', a custom black metal staircase rises to the second floor. There, pulling the facade treatment inside, the battens stand in vertical rows, interlocking with the ceiling battens to create more flexible display surfaces.

MASQUESPACIO takes cues from the angle of smartphone screens in a contemporary take on repair shops

VALENCIA — Local creative consultant Masquespacio had re-hauled smartphone repair brand Doctor Manzana and designed its first store in 2013. For its second space, located in the city's University district, they brought back the idea of mixing an industrial repair shop with a doctor's office. Both designs are based largely on the 54-degree angle of touchscreens, which was applied graphically and organisationally to the new face of the brand and the interior design.

The second location was designed in the spirit of the first, in order to maintain and build on the successful brand identity, which is already recognised by the clientele. Both spaces share much of the same materials, the 54-degree angles, and colour scheme: green and blue are used as a reference to medical clinics, salmon to fashionistas and purple to tech geeks.

To keep things fresh, however, in the newest space a greater emphasis was placed on metal finishes that lend the shop an industrial quality, recalling a laboratory. Another addition is a space dedicated to workshops and lectures in a room distinct from the sales floor and repair. It is furnished with Masquespacio's Doctor Workshop high stool and chair, which became the first product sold directly through the studio under the sub-brand name Mas Creations.

RIGHT Colour blocking of the space is based on the 54-degree angle of smartphone screens, with each colour representing an aspect of the business: salmon for fashionistas and blue for repair areas, for example.

Luis Beltran

Masquespacio
DOCTOR MANZANA

NEW YORK SWEETS

Minas Kosmidis
[Architecture in Concept]

NEW YORK SWEETS

MINAS KOSMIDIS [ARCHITECTURE IN CONCEPT] brings a slice of the big apple to Cyprus for a local patisserie

NICOSIA — As the name suggests, New York Sweets is a baker of American-inspired treats. Minas Kosmidis [Architecture in Concept] was asked to renovate the chain's flagship store with a design that reflects its status as a family owned company while redefining the brand's aesthetic identity.

The Greek design firm responded with a concept that transports customers straight to the Big Apple. An All-American welcome is provided by the building's facade, whose horizontal canopies recall the entrances to New York's landmark buildings. Inside, references to the city range from the subtle to spectacular. While most customers will look at the pastries, they might miss the fact that the layout of the free-standing display showcases and counters is reminiscent of Manhattan's grid-like street patterns, while the positioning of pastries inside the displays corresponds to a bird's eye view of the borough.

Nonetheless, there's no missing the tribute to the city's skyline on the back wall, in which marble blocks combine to form a panorama of the city's iconic skyscrapers. The metal blades that separate each marble formation are more than decorative — as well as giving the impression of more height in the low space, architect Ismini Chrysochoou reveals that they are intended to recall the edges of New York's high rise buildings as seen from the ground.

ABOVE The store's low ceilings are offset by a series of metallic blades placed irregularly around the walls to give the impression of more height.

RIGHT A liberal use of marble and skyscraper silhouettes recreate New York's art-deco heyday.

THE LAYOUT OF FREESTANDING DISPLAYS AND COUNTERS IS REMINISCENT OF MANHATTAN'S GRID-LIKE STREET PATTERNS

MVRDV

BULGARI

MVRDV reinterprets a luxury brand's heritage by experimenting with traditional materials

KUALA LUMPUR — MVRDV designed the facade of this 103-m^2 Bulgari flagship, which will serve as the first in a series of material-pioneering storefronts for the luxury brand. The Dutch studio drew on the brand's heritage, referencing the iconic cornice of the via Condotti shop in Rome, which is repeated asymmetrically. Simultaneously, their design is a contemporary expression of the fashion house in that it was created by experimenting with, and innovating on, traditional materials.

During the day, passers-by and visitors inside the store can see the facade's seemingly 'organic materiality', which resembles veiny marble or cracking volcanic stone. It is actually made from pale grey fibre-reinforced concrete (Glass Reinforced Concrete or GRC) cut according to a pattern and filled with 15-mm-thick amber-coloured epoxy resin lit with LEDs. Stainless steel sheets serve as a foundation for the resin and panel joints are cleverly concealed by incorporating them into the vein pattern. This cladding is actually an entirely new product that was developed in collaboration with Technical University Delft, and Tensoforma. At night, the appearance of the whole building shifts dramatically as the light glows like magma about to burst the seams of the facade.

Daria Scagliola

LEFT By day and night, the facade expresses different effects around its curious materiality. During the day, it resembles a veined marble but at night, the contrast between opacity and luminous translucence is amplified dramatically.

ABOVE The windows feature two layers of 8 mm decorative glass that were laminated with a film of polyvinyl butyral (PVB) and a coloured membrane in an amber gradient, and then set into 5 mm brushed brass side profiles and sill.

Nong Studio
V2 BOUTIQUE

NONG STUDIO interprets a brand's DNA through colour, shape and texture

SHANGHAI — V2's first boutique in China's largest city is situated in a traditional Shanghainese Shikumen in Xintiandi, a district that is filled with high-end fashion stores and lifestyle boutiques. To make the space stand out among its new neighbours, Nong Studio decided to retain the building's residential aspect and design a boutique that feels like home.

The brand was keen that the interior should play with its three key brand elements: colour, shape and texture. The Shanghai-based design firm's response was to create a girl's secret closet, a cosy space that offers respite from the world outside and somewhere to admire her favourite things: in this case, an array of beautiful handbags. These are showcased in compartmented long shelves that extend through the wall into a mirror reflection to add a touch of magic.

Gentle pastel pink sets the tone for a comfortable space, with flourishes like a feather boa covered pole in the window to establish the effect of a dressup room. A mix of classic and contemporary touches suggests that all ages are at home here: vintage mirrors, velvet cushions and art-deco floor tiling are matched by stainless steel surfaces. Further sanctuary is offered on the second floor, an open-plan space that uses a French window and skylight to optimise natural light while offering customers privacy and comfort.

A MIX OF CLASSIC AND CONTEMPORARY TOUCHES SUGGESTS THAT ALL AGES ARE AT HOME

Patricia Parinejad

Ohlab
IN-SIGHT

An optical illusion by OHLAB is as practical as it is spectacular

MIAMI — Sometimes a brand's name or logo is a creative brief in itself. OHLAB could claim both of these as inspiration for its design of the In-Sight concept store in Miami, Florida. The clothing curator's logo is a pair of binoculars, a visual device that the Palma-based designers translated into a series of 24 white wooden panels placed in parallel along the length of the room. When viewed from the outside (and through the binoculars stencilled on the shop windows), these stretch out to form a tunnel, which thanks to the angles of each cut-out panel, appears to slowly rotate throughout the space. At the end of the store, a graphic panel with a trompe-l'oeil gives the impression that the panels continue to infinity and beyond.

The gaps between the panels can be used for a variety of purposes, from product exhibition, storage to simply sitting down. Customers get a hint of what each alcove has to often thanks to the angle of each panel. Despite the intricacy of the design, the panel's construction system is surprisingly simple. As they were made in Spain the system had to be easy to take apart and put together upon arrival in the US — especially as construction time was only three weeks.

LEFT A graphic panel at the back of the store features a trompe-l'oeil that creates an illusion that extends the illusion beyond the store limits.

RIGHT Through the extrusion, translation and rotation of the logo, an imaginary volume is created.

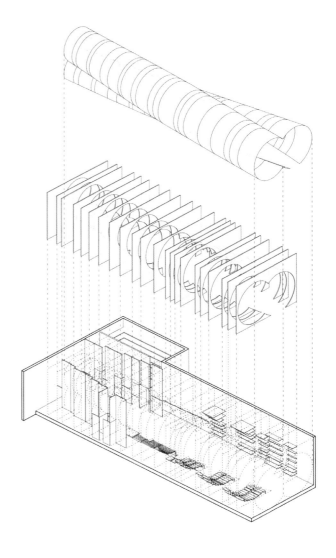

GAPS BETWEEN THE
PANELS CAN BE USED FOR
PRODUCT EXHIBITION,
STORAGE OR SEATING

Courtesy of Herschel Supply

OMER ARBEL translates brand values into spatial design and art

VANCOUVER — Canadian designer and artist Omer Arbel translated three themes into one interior to create the 465-m² flagship for accessories and apparel brand Herschel Supply. Arbel used heritage maple floor boards that continue up some of the walls, dressed the fitting rooms in marble and whitewashed existing brick walls and heritage tin ceiling tiles. Cast aluminium furniture was chosen to match the spirit of the exuberant, frothy aluminium sculpture designed by the artist for the space.

The 'Herschel Forever' theme, which explores the precipitous growth of the brand across cultures and markets, was translated into a spatial design. The theme is represented in the use of one and two-way mirrors and other optical devices, along with meticulously controlled light levels, to proliferate the reflections of stacked Herschel products into infinity. Another theme translated into the store was 'You = Me = Herschel', which stems from the brand's commitment to equality and community. To visualise these values, the team commissioned multiple figurative sculptures from various artists and placed them together at the centre of the space. Finally, 'Here, There, Herschel' interprets the brand's attitude toward the global community and travel. The designers mounted screens around the shop to capture daily 'non-events' in far-flung places that remind visitors of the coexistence of other peoples and cultures both remote and neighbouring.

LEFT Arbel is the creative director of Canadian lighting brand Bocci, whose products illuminate the store, but Arbel also sand-cast 44, an aluminium sculpture that exists symbiotically with the resin cash desk and planters arranged throughout the space.

BELOW For the accessories and apparel brand, sculptural garment racks and wall-mounted hooks are in the spirit of the artwork that populates the store.

LET'S TALK ABOUT US

Omer Arbel Office
HERSCHEL SUPPLY GASTOWN

Pattern Studio
THE DAILY EDITED

Sean Fennessey

tde.

An online store is given a feminine but futuristic physical makeover by PATTERN STUDIO

MELBOURNE — What's the best way to translate a successful e-commerce brand into the realm of bricks and mortar? Australian design firm Pattern Studio decided the best course of action for The Daily Edited, a purveyor of customisable luxury fashion accessories, would be to pay tribute to its online roots while offering a sensual retail experience that makes the most of its physical presence.

The outcome is a feminine but futuristic flagship store that immerses visitors in the brand's personality. Customers are swept inside by a curved entrance that announces the store's subtle space-age aesthetics of rounded lines and recessed lighting. A restrained colour palette of white terrazzo and Norwegian rose marble is dominated by terracotta pink, a shade chosen for its status as the brand colour, not (solely) for any feminine-friendly overtones.

As the brand has a more accessible price point than most luxury labels, the store design had to incorporate more product displays than is usual in the sector — but without making the interior feel cheap, cluttered or overly commercial. Pattern Studio's solution was to balance concentrated product displays with merchandise-free areas. These are given space to breathe in a minimal interior in which furniture is limited to a natural stone table and point of sale bench whose sculptural aesthetics make desirable objects in themselves.

CUSTOMERS ARE SWEPT INSIDE BY A CURVED ENTRANCE THAT ANNOUNCES THE STORE'S SUBTLE SPACE-AGE AESTHETICS

Sean Fennessey

PREVIOIUS SPREAD The store's sophisticated atmosphere is intended to increase
The Daily Edited's appeal to a wider, more
discerning demographic.

BELOW Two freestanding elements act as
anchors around which customers can flow
freely around the boutique.

SCHEMATA ARCHITECTS turns constraint into opportunity by using a moving vertical display

NAGOYA — For Descente Blanc Nagoya's inaugural shop-in-shop, Schemata Architects began by taking advantage of the site's shallow but broad retail floor, suspending rows of vertically moving display systems across the entire width of the store. Jackets, hoodies and puffers are displayed in tight-packed rows which can be lowered to about half a metre off the floor, or kept up within the disguised double-height ceiling, leaving the trowelled masonry floor beneath them entirely clear.

If the latter is the case, walking into the store from the corridor, shoppers at first see only the bottom hems of the jackets overhead until, having fully entered, they find that the ceiling above them is a sea of garments. When the displays are down, however, they fill the entire width of the store, so that both staff and customers use part of the corridor that runs along the storefront as a way to circulate through the retail floor, blurring the boundary between commercial and public space. According to the architects, this subtle tool, along with the generous emptiness of the shop floor, 'creates an inviting atmosphere where shoppers feel welcomed.'

RIGHT Schemata made a virtue of the shop's shallow, broad retail floor, instead of considering it a constraint. They hung garments from the ceiling, across the entire width of the floor, on industrial steel poles.

FOLLOWING SPREAD At the main entrance, where the ceiling is double-height, the architects also displayed jackets and anoraks in tight-packed rows of vertically moving display systems, leaving the floor under them empty. Passers-by see only the bottom hem of the clothes from the corridor.

Kenta Hasegawa

Schemata Architects
DESCENTE BLANC NAGOYA

THE BLURRING OF COMMERCIAL
AND PUBLIC SPACE CREATES AN
INVITING ATMOSPHERE WHERE
SHOPPERS FEEL WELCOMED

DESCENTE BLANC

Sergio Mannino Studio
GLAM SEAMLESS

SERGIO MANNINO translates an online hair salon into an ethereal bricks and mortar business

NEW YORK — At a time when the hair extensions market is growing, this is Glam Seamless' first bricks and mortar salon. Until the store was commissioned, it had been exclusively an e-commerce site. Today, the 176-m² store in Soho gives customers the opportunity to experience products directly.

Online, the brand is pink and white, with an emphasis on glamour, so these were the first cues that designer Sergio Mannino and Martina Guandalini used to manifest the Glam persona — feminine, bold, dreamy — in physical space. This also determined the colour scheme — smooth cream and millennial pink — and character of the space: the store is divided into two areas, the sales area and the salon itself via string curtains in a gradient of white to pink. 'The curtains reminded us of the lightness and softness of hair,' says Mannino. What is more, they contrast with the 'modern/retro-inspired' silhouettes of the furnishings. These purpose-made counters and displays were fabricated in transparent glass, white lacquer and hand-made blush pink terrazzo tiles by 1925 srl.

According to the design team, using the brand's core colours was a challenge because they tend to make a space feel childish. To find a balance, the team used the blond wooden floor, glass, the sophisticated texture of the terrazzo tiles and bold shapes like the globe pendant lighting and bespoke mirrors.

RIGHT The curtains partition the busier sales and more tranquil salon sides of the store, essentially serving as glamorous decorative scenery flats.

FOLLOWING SPREAD The rose tinted colour palette found its counterpoint in robust forms and sophisticated materials.

make every day
GLAMOROUS

Superfuturedesign*
MASEL

Gabriele Gualdi, Superfuturedesign

A small store is made to feel big through innovative use of colour and space by SUPERFUTUREDESIGN*

MILAN — Size may not be everything, but having to work with just 25-m^2 certainly posed a considerable challenge to Superfuturedesign*. To make the most of this limited space, the Dubai-based design firm implemented a dynamic concept that befits the classic but innovative character of the brand it houses: Masel, an artisanal maker of personalised silk ties and pocket squares.

The design team felt that the original storefront had a touch of old-fashioned English character about it that matched the gentleman's accessories found within, and therefore decided to channel this influence into the interior. A deep dark blue is used both inside and out to set the tone for a boutique that has a distinct naval feel. This impression is generated by a display table that's reminiscent of an old shipping crate and the many ropes that line the walls and ceiling. As the ropes criss-cross the space, they generate both depth and movement to make the room feel bigger and add tension. Wooden rings peep out from behind the ropes to display Masel's flamboyant ties, pocket squares and assorted accessories. The contrast between the restrained tones of the rope and the flamboyant products results in splashes of colour that jump out at potential customers.

LEFT Masel may be in Milan, but a hint of old-fashioned English in the original facade is a perfect match for the brand's handmade gentleman's accessories.

FOLLOWING SPREAD The subdued colours of the ropes form the ideal background for the vibrant neckties to stand out dramatically.

POWERSHOP 6

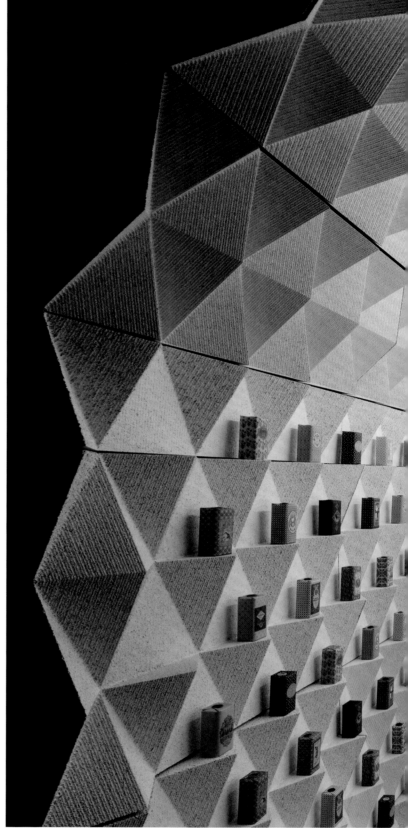

Eric Petschek

TACKLEBOX ARCHITECTURE
honours the heritage of a fragrance brand through references to Portugal's architecture and craft traditions

NEW YORK — Architect Jeremy Barbour was recognised early on for a formally and materially clever shop he designed using only paper bags. More recently, he has crafted a 50-m² shop, on the ground floor of an early 19th-century building on Elizabeth Street in Soho, from custom-milled cork tiles. At its heart, the first international store for a 131-year-old Portuguese beauty and fragrance brand, the space is a faceted gem.

Drawing in passers-by through the window and giving a tip of the hat to Portuguese architecture and craftsmanship, a 13-m-long freestanding custom cork archway runs perpendicular to the street just inside a large glazed storefront. Bottles of scent rest on small shelves inside niches carved out of the inner walls of the arch, while the 1500 diamond-shaped cork panels extend slightly inward like scales. Milled from sustainably harvested Portuguese cork, the tiles were inspired by the tiled facade of Lisbon's historic Casa dos Bicos.

The tunnel, itself, refers to the arched doorways and elaborate *azulejo* tile work in the arrival hall at Porto's São Bento train station, depicting historical events and welcoming visitors to the city. The station was commissioned in 1887, the same year that the brand was founded, making the archway a portal into both Portuguese culture and the brand.

Tacklebox Architecture
CLAUS PORTO

PREVIOUS SPREAD Niches in the arch showcase the soaps and fragrance bottles. The arcade serves as a gateway into the Portuguese culture, as well as the heritage brand and its perfumes.

ABOVE A wash basin anchors the space, alluding to a baptismal font and the ritual of daily cleansing. It was carved from the same block of Estremoz marble as the washbasin in Claus Porto's flagship Portuguese store.

RIGHT Barbour had 1500 diamond-shaped cork panels milled from sustainably harvested Portuguese cork. It took under 10 days to assemble it inside the storefront.

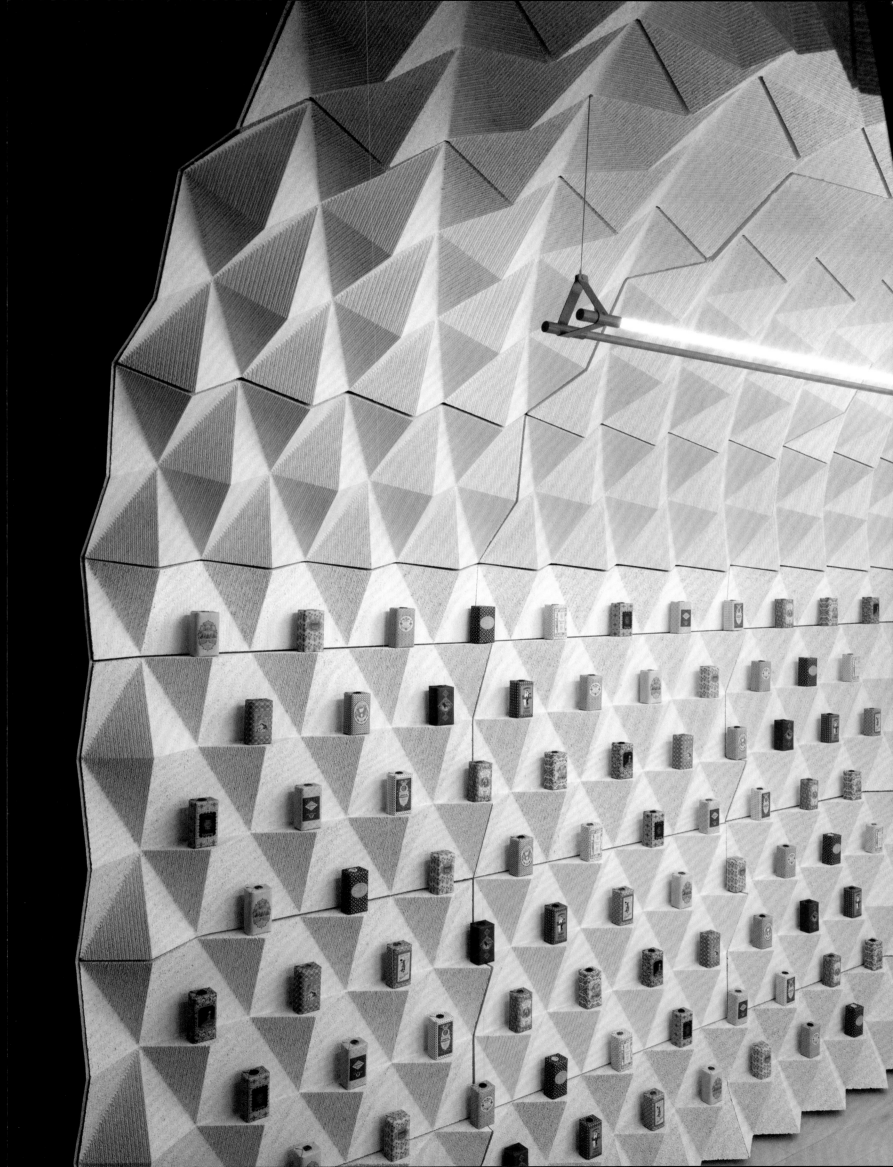

Tchai
DHL EXPRESS

Jaap Vliegenthart

TCHAI creates a dynamic, scalable retail experience that places visitors at the heart of the brand

AMSTERDAM — In recent years, the consumer market and retail space have become increasingly important to international shipper DHL. In a succinct 100-m², Tchai's modular retail concept, scalable to any store size desired, immediately immerses visitors in the brand's logistical story through crisp, clear visuals. At the same time, it emphasises the courier's commitment to quick, easy, reliable, pleasant service through the shop experience, itself.

White paint and a concrete floor frame brand colours — yellow and burgundy — as well as a wood veneer counter at the back. Behind the counter, a full scale photograph of the cargo bay of an airliner makes it look as if packages are rolling straight into the airplane on a conveyor belt. Tchai's interior visualises core brand components: the open, flowing space demonstrates its transparency, reliability, quality of service and ease-of-use while broadcasting the idea that it 'delivers joy'. Making it clear where to drop packages and find labels and pre-folded DHL Express easy boxes, the space also offers free coffee, Wi-Fi, phone charging, and seating.

The most unusual service? A gift-wrap counter where visitors can wrap presents after receiving them, or before sending them, as parcels. It is another clever detail demonstrating the brand's belief that how customers feel after leaving the store is linked inextricably to the experience they have in the shop.

LEFT Like a tiny museum, three showcases tell the brand story. LED spotlights create focal points and reinforce circulation while cargo containers clad the ceiling and walls.

FOLLOWING SPREAD LEFT Passers-by and visitors to the store are greeted by a DHL courier bike on display in the storefront, representing the 'last mile' or last means of transport that completes their 'green' delivery cycle.

FOLLOWING SPREAD RIGHT Parcels placed on a conveyor belt in-between the rear counters appear to roll into the belly of a DHL cargo plane, which is rendered at actual scale on a wall mural behind the counter, obscuring a door to a staff area.

IN A SUCCINCT 100-M², A MODULAR RETAIL CONCEPT IMMEDIATELY IMMERSES VISITORS IN THE BRAND'S HISTORY

Moritz Bernoully

Zeller & Moye
TROQUER FASHION HOUSE

ZELLER & MOYE tucked a golden forest of fashion into an intriguing black box building

MEXICO CITY — In the central district of Polanco, Zeller & Moye designed online fashion retailer Troquer's 230-m² storage-on-view space, where online customers may visit the warehouse to experience products in person.

The designers began by refurbishing an existing 1960s residence — visitors must still ring the bell to be let in — painting it in an 'introverted' matte black. To create a luxurious space for display, instead of sales, the studio settled on a low-budget solution. A limited palette of raw industrial materials, including gold-anodised extruded aluminium profiles and metal sheet for garment racks and shelves, and solid black rubber for flooring. The entire forest-like display is custom-designed and grows to fill the perimeters and corners of the room. Connected and stacked, the metal tubes produce a dynamic lattice of verticals and horizontals of varying heights and density, which are reflected overhead in the form of bespoke vertical LED light fixtures.

Dresses are shown on custom-made golden hangers, while slender metal sheets rest on the grid at various heights to provide shelves for bags, shoes and other accessories. All horizontal bars can serve as clothing rails, which generates infinite potential reconfigurations of the display. This means that, since the stored clothes are constantly moved around, repeat visitors can experience a different composition almost daily, deepening ties to the brand.

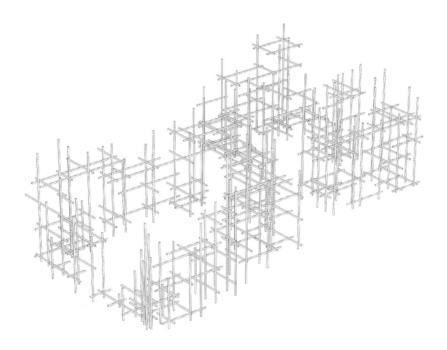

PREVIOUS SPREAD LEFT The online fashion brand's storage-on-view location consists of racks and shelves that appear to 'grow' through the space, their linearity and verticality reflected in bespoke LED lights suspended overhead.

PREVIOUS SPREAD RIGHT The display furniture is made from gold-anodized extruded aluminium profiles and sheets that form an asymmetrical, branching, contiguous structure that fills the perimeters and corners of each room as well as the storefront (formerly the garage).

LEFT Fitted together and stacked to form a lattice-work of racks and surfaces at various heights, depths and densities, the system incorporates mirrors, as well. A solid black rubber floor, which also climbs the stairs, unifies all rooms.

THE MEDIUM IS THE MESSAGE

RETAIL SPACE AS A STORYTELLING DEVICE

Interview

GEORG THIERSCH

GEORG THIERSCH, co-founder of Munich-based design studio 1zu33, considers the importance of creating tangible touchpoints between the brand and the consumer in order to realise relevant retail experiences.

What is 1zu33's approach to retail space design? We strive to create distinct and highly recognisable spaces that at once build on the brand/customer relationship and provide a unique retail experience.

What, in your opinion, is the main goal of retail spaces today? The main goal of retail spaces used to be to sell goods. While this is still a key factor, there is also the need to make a brand tangible, visible and emotionally-embraceable through a physical space. Conceptual interior design offers a wide range of tools to specifically orchestrate the environment in which to communicate the various features of a brand.

Wherever possible, retail spaces should try to establish a connection between customers and the brand that goes beyond the product or service. To experience the unique character of a brand and how it appears in a specific location — for example, by revealing information about history or craft — allows customers to connect with the store on a much deeper level. This personal connection is the goal.

The projects in this chapter tell a panoply of stories, from the history of a store's location, to appropriating the symbols of cities or a product's key elements. Why do you think this approach to retail spaces as storytelling devices is successful? Some customers might only focus on hard facts such as product, price and service, but most human beings are open to embrace a holistic spatial experience and able to transform this experience into something memorable; a true connection.

We believe the approach to establish this true connection between customers and brands should be based on multiple levels: the more tangible touchpoints between brand and consumer are established within a store, the higher is the chance to make customers feel something relevant.

'THE KEY TO ESTABLISH CUSTOMER ENGAGEMENT IS TO PURSUE AN EMOTIONAL, ALMOST SUBCONSCIOUS CONNECTION'

How can you use these narratives to engage customers in the store experience? These narrative elements offer strong connection points within the spatial experience of retail environments. The nature of these connection points can range from brand-relevant stories to very local, almost personal aspects. Whatever element is used, the key to establish customer engagement is to pursue an emotional, almost subconscious connection.

How would you define a successful retail design? For us one of the most important aspects is to ensure that the design merges the very local, functional and cultural requirements of retail environments with the brand's most central corporate philosophy and expectations. In other words, designers need to establish a sensitive, well-informed, rational and contextual design strategy in order to carefully choreograph and control every feature of the retail experience.

How do you envision the future of retail design? Most brands have realised how important it is to provide tangible retail spaces that build on their credibility and emotionally engage customers. Retail design has a great future when it comes to high-profile projects.

1zu33
AESOP NIKOLAISTRASSE

1ZU33 layers a city's contrasting historical, political and cultural references

LEIPZIG — In only 95-m², Munich-based architecture firm 1zu33 layered a Aesop store with references to the sophisticated history of a city that, for hundreds of years, has been celebrated as an epicentre of printing, the arts and cultural events, including the oldest book fair in the world.

The designers, who had already done Aesop interiors in Munich, Stuttgart and Hannover, referenced the aesthetics and political context behind the prefabricated designs of the former German Democratic Republic for the brand's first location in Leipzig. The studio then added contemporary elements referring to the city's post-reunification development. Although visually rich in contrast, colour, texture and form, the interior relies on a limited palette of materials, resonating with an almost sacred sense of sparseness.

The Nikolaistrasse storefront opens onto a glossy screed floor, green and grey colour scheme and green velvet wall panels. Powder-coated metal shelving backed with translucent glass bricks, and a simple industrial-looking desk lamp, allude to the city's industrial homogeneity during Germany's East/West division. Striking a warm contrast, the sales counter, crafted from oiled plywood with rounded edges, assumes an obtuse L-shape that turns obliquely, even coyly, from the door. The shop, behind a coarse concrete facade guarded by swaddled cherubs, is a lush and intriguing environment.

PREVIOUS SPREAD The designers chose warm tones of green and grey, which are visible through a storefront set into a rough time-worn facade.

BELOW An industrial look is balanced by wooden furnishings with rounded edges and an elegant post-war look and feel, like the signature Aesop sink visible from the kerb.

RIGHT The space is defined by powder-coated metal shelves that curve around the room backed with clear glass brick.

Using theatre conventions and perfume notes, 1ZU33 designs a stage for rare scents

MUNICH — Owner Eva Bogner has devoted the 90-m^2 boutique Parfums Uniques entirely to uncommon perfumes and the staging of intense, sophisticated olfactory experiences. Around an experience that is visceral, emotional, intuitive and difficult to define or even describe, local architecture studio 1zu33 has created a space of great clarity.

The meticulously curated inventory of exclusive, limited edition fragrances is displayed in three zones inspired by theatre conventions and the three phases of scent perception and design. The top note, the most immediate and evanescent element of a fragrance when it is applied or sniffed, is represented by the space that opens upward through lighting. A large brass plinth in the front of the store, visible immediately from the kerb, represents the heart note, the scent of a perfume that surfaces just as the most ephemeral top notes are dissipating. The base notes are represented by linoleum-coated furnishings and bare terraced podiums on which bottles are 'staged' like works of art. In the rear, a darker, more intimate private room featuring textile surfaces and soft furniture serves as a sanctuary of scent where aromatic candles play the protagonist.

RIGHT The core of the store, unusual perfume bottles are displayed like artworks on a cascading series of linoleum-clad plinths.

FOLLOWING SPREAD A massive brass display podium can be seen from the street and symbolizes the middle or heart note, which emerges just as the flighty top notes evaporate.

David Koplin

1zu33
PARFUMS UNIQUES

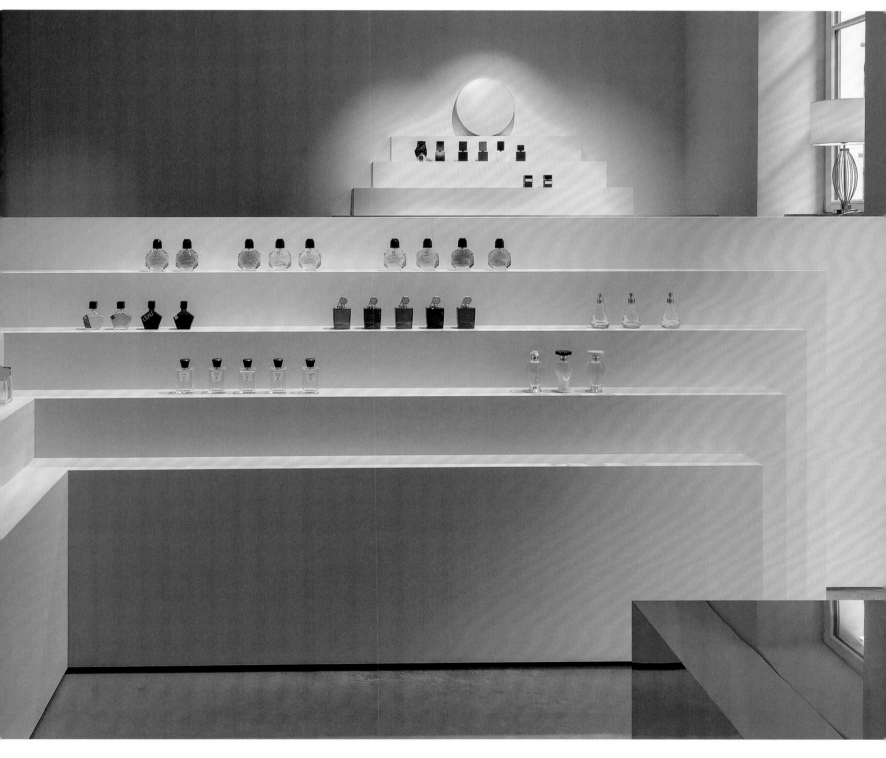

AROUND AN EXPERIENCE THAT IS DIFFICULT TO DEFINE
THE TEAM DESIGNED A SPACE OF GREAT CLARITY

Dennis Lo

A Work of Substance
KHROMIS

A WORK OF SUBSTANCE sculpts an eyewear boutique to help visitors better experience light

HONG KONG — To design a shop that would highlight the function and value of the product sold there, local studio A Work of Substance imagined this 75-m² sunglass boutique as a showcase of light by multiple means. The interior represents the studio's exploration of micro and macro light, reflection and refraction, through a clever use of materials that invoke the full participation of its visitors' senses. The designers sought materials that would transmit, focus and diffuse light, including stainless steel, mirror, acrylic, glass and even bright white (eco-friendly) paint. Three large windows, featuring elegantly rounded corners, bring light into the corner shop. This radius is repeated in multiple ways indoors and out: in doorways and passageways, multifunctional niches, and in furniture.

The store's flexible wall display system is made up of small, clear acrylic shelves slot into backlit grids of steel. The design team framed these reflective/refractive surfaces with luxurious reclaimed timber, while the sides of display tables, points of sale, and even a small coffee bar, were repeatedly and deeply chamfered. An example of craftsmanship of the highest standard, the chamfering recalls the shape of stacked prisms. The wood also gives the eyes a moment's rest from the shop's play of light.

ABOVE Located on an exposed street corner, the sunglass shop uses large windows to draw in natural light.

BELOW The wooden flanks of furnishings like displays and point of sales counters are chamfered to resemble opaque prisms and to conceal display or storage drawers.

RIGHT In an arched, steel-lined niche, visitors can sit and try glasses on as if at a vanity.

FOLLOWING SPREAD The wall display system is a grid of stainless steel into which acrylic shelves are slotted and illuminated from behind, forming a dynamic, yet neutral background for the sunglasses.

Ædifica

MAISON BIRKS

Ben Rahn, A Frame

ABOVE By creating an atmosphere of casual luxury the designers aim to entice young shoppers who might be intimidated by traditional jewellery stores.

LEFT An elegant combination of natural oak, walnut and stones highlights the quality and craftsmanship of the products on sale.

ÆDIFICA's crystal clear concept aims to attract millennials to a jewellery store

TORONTO — Birks is one of Canada's most famous jewellers, with a proud history stretching back to 1879. Aware that many young people can be put off by the reserved formality of a traditional jewellery store, Birks wanted to offer millennials a more welcoming environment. Therefore, Montreal-based studio Ædifica conceived an open design that removes any barriers between sales staff and customers.

The first step was to ensure that passers-by could see directly into Maison Birks. Large windows straddle two corners of the diamond-like facade to offer a clear view into almost every part of the store. Once inside, the store layout has been organised to put customers immediately at ease. Staff don't stand stiffly behind high counters but move freely around to engage with customers. A variety of themed pods and stations (a bridal bar, a wall of pearls) offer casual seating options for visitors to sit down and view jewellery in comfort.

There's still space for some traditional touches — natural oak, walnut, stone and steel feature prominently in the decor — especially to highlight Birks' heritage. As much as informing customers about the brand's story, it's necessary to create a strong visual identity. Retail areas in the store are divided between third party shop-in-shops and Birks' own products. The latter are given prominence and context with a display of vintage photos highlighting the company's history and a wall featuring a collection of the brand's iconic blue gift boxes.

Arket
004002 – 941

Courtesy of Arket

ABOVE Linear light fixtures, which parallel garment-accenting spotlight tracks, serve as ambient lighting. The architects ensured that all windows remain exposed to maximise daylight entering the space, while a historic skylight in the atrium also offers natural illumination.

RIGHT The speckled grey terrazzo flooring makes it look as if a thick fog were dissipating at one's feet, also helping to keep visitors alert and focused on the merchandise.

FOLLOWING SPREAD Preserving the existing building's 19th-century historical details, the store is modeled on a historical archive.

Monochrome timelessness reigns in ARKET's fashion archive

COPENHAGEN – The first store of clothing and houseware brand Arket, a daughter brand of H&M Group, opened on the ground floor of a historical former post office. Selling items designed by an in-house team alongside cherry-picked products by other brands, the shop also includes a seasonal café serving menus in line with the New Nordic Food Manifesto.

Unlike those of its parent brand, Arket's products are 'made to be used and loved for a long time', which makes it apt that the designers preserved the look and feel of the grand old building and then modeled the interiors on a classical historical archive. Even the store's name, 004002 – 941, recalls old filing system nomenclature.

The interiors feature arches, columns and moldings, copious cubbyhole shelving, reading tables and even paper filing trays typical of a classical archive, but take on a futuristic, or even timeless, look because they are painted almost entirely grey. Grey walls, grey ceiling, grey ductwork and grey terrazzo-printed recycled carpet all serve to make the rooms feel monolithic. Most importantly, the store's monochrome lining serves to throw the merchandise into sharp, colourful focus.

Bel Epok

SPITZENHAUS

BEL EPOK fills a perfumery in a listed building with the scent of change

ZURICH — Listed buildings may be beautiful but they do throw up design challenges, as Bel Epok discovered when asked to outfit a perfumery in Zurich. The German design firm's intervention had to comply with local Swiss renovation guidelines for landmark sites. In practical terms, this meant that the original wood flooring and the egg-and-dart moulding on the built-in cabinets could not be touched, a status that restricted the potential range of colours.

As a result, Bel Epok decided to make the site's history a key part of their concept. A warm grey colour scheme respects the original fittings, with flashes of green signifying the contemporary flourishes that have been added. For example, the sleek sales counters have a classical tone, but the use of glass and steel brings them firmly into the 21st century. The two eras meet in the freestanding stone curtains in front of the large store windows, whose appearance of unrolled bolts of fabric pays tribute to the neighbourhood's 19th-century status as a textile shop area. This combination demonstrates the studio's goal of creating 'a unique and inspiring shopping environment that combines the solid splendour of a bygone era with the bright, clean and airy ease of today.'

ABOVE As the stockroom isn't accessible from the sales floor, the counter displays incorporate plenty of storage space.

RIGHT A key design challenge for Bel Epok was the client's need for specific brand presentations to be integrated into a unified concept.

CBA Clemens Bachmann Architekten
KOPPELMANN OPTIK

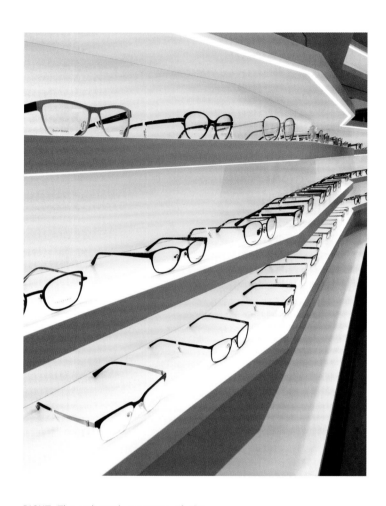

CBA's colour coding system creates clear zones for customers and staff in an eyewear store

GELTERKINDEN — Lines of sight are important in any retail environment, but perhaps particularly relevant for an optician. CBA were asked to redesign Koppelmann Optik to create a zoning system with clear presentation and customer areas. The key to this was a subtle colour scheme: white for products, green for customers.

In the fit out, glasses are displayed on a white sculptural shelf that zigzags along one wall. As the shelves jut out into the room, they open up different perspectives and draw customers further into the store. By placing the glasses on a white, brightly lit background, the designers ensure that the colours of the frames pop out at the customer.

The tables at the centre of the space are where the two colours collide: like the shelves, the tables are white and angular, but there is a recess for potted plants and the large carpet underneath each table is green. Greenery is also liberally used at the front of the store and the back, where a moss wall marks the small lounge and waiting area. Boundaries between the customer and product zones are subtly indicated by a row of birch trunks that create privacy between the passageway and consultation tables, while functional rooms including the workshop are located in a separate area at the back.

RIGHT The polygonal geometry of the shelves mounted on two walls opens the room up in different directions.

ABOVE The shelving system has no pre-defined places for eyewear, creating increased possibilities for product presentation.

A portable retail solution by CHRISTOPHER WARD STUDIO can be integrated anywhere

NOVENTA DI PIAVE — Despite all appearances to the contrary, you're not looking at a fixed shop interior, but a portable retail solution. As much as a design concept that could be integrated in a variety of locations, Italian fashion brand Aniye By wanted a practical solution that would reduce production costs and assembly times. With this in mind, Christopher Ward Studio designed a box in a box, an all-in-one package that contains the necessary furniture and lighting fixtures.

The basis is a white metal cage that acts as both lighting rig and store boundaries. Once erected, it demarcates a new environment and renders the character of the original space irrelevant. The freestanding elements that stand within the cage, such as clothing rails and tables, have all been designed with round lines to play off the cage's strict geometry. A contradictory variety of materials add further visual depth: white metal serves as the neutral line between golden brass fittings which stand in stark contrast to the OSB used for the tables, a material that is most often used in industrial projects. The final playful touch is a liberal use of plants throughout the space. Not only does the greenery break up the host interior's lines, straight or otherwise, it also serves as a colourful antidote to the white metal cage.

RIGHT Tables and clothing racks were designed with round lines to offset the right angles of the metal cage.

FOLLOWING SPREAD Materials were chosen to be deliberately contradictory. Elegant golden brass towers above OSB blocks in an environment that, thanks to the white metal used throughout the store, remains harmonious.

Christopher Ward Studio
ANIYE BY

Davide Galli

A WHITE METAL CAGE ACTS AS BOTH LIGHTING RIG AND STORE BOUNDARIES

CLOU architects
JEWELLERY BOX CHAOWAI

CLOU ARCHITECTS envisions a modern reinterpretation of 1920s art-deco department stores

BEIJING — The original brief for Jewellery Box Chaowai was to design a high-end boutique. However, given the scale of the project (it is spread over three storeys and comprises 3200-m² of jewellery boutiques and 400 metres of jewellery counters for individual vendors), CLOU architects felt that a department store look and feel might be more appropriate. 'We looked at art-deco department store interiors like the Bullocks Wilshire Perfume Hall in Los Angeles for inspiration,' says Christian Taeubert, director of the local studio. 'We picked two of the time's characteristic materials — natural stone and stainless steel — which helped us create a modernized sense of opulence which would not be thought of as vintage.'

To create a sense of unity throughout the house, counters were fitted with anodized, corrugated steel and customised in a range of tones and natural stone selections to create a different atmosphere on each floor. Each of which hosts different precious stones, the lighting and materials have been selected to show the jewellery in an optimal way. For example, diamonds on the ground floor require cold lighting, which is balanced by gold column cladding and signage boxes. On the second floor, jade jewellery, which requires warmer light, is offset by darker material finishes.

RIGHT Display materials were carefully chosen to best show off each kind of precious stone. On the second floor, jade shines bright against a dark background.

FOLLOWING SPREAD In order to accommodate individual vendors in Jewellery Box Chaowai, the team implemented linear counter layouts inspired by classic American department stores.

LIGHTING AND
MATERIALS ON
EACH FLOOR
HAVE BEEN
SELECTED TO
SHOW OFF EACH
KIND OF STONE
IN THE BEST WAY

中钢黄金

Creative Studio Unravel
IMMI

CREATIVE STUDIO UNRAVEL critiques industrial dogmas of beauty in a space that celebrates the birth of a new era in Chinese fashion

SHANGHAI — Two-year-old Chinese fashion brand IMMI gave birth to its first 160-m^2 flagship store in the shopping district of Xintiandi. In part, the interior design centred on this notion of birth and the birth canal to tell a story about the origins of a new brand and as an analogue to a new phase of redoubled creativity in the Chinese fashion industry. Creative Studio Unravel used the metaphor of the railroad to allow the space to change from day-to-day — almost as quickly as China's retail landscape — but also as a critique of industrial dogmas.

The womb is articulated through a series of red surfaces: opaque, glossy acrylic walls form volumes that serve as convertible displays and define sections of the store by apparel type. The railroad, on the other hand, is represented via a series of stainless steel carts in various sizes and shapes, which are set into tracks in the floor. The carts lend motion to the space, while allowing it to function dynamically, replacing static displays with movable ones that give the space flexibility. Abstracted, irregular authorless objects piled on the carts represent 'creative creatures born in the mother's womb' and are intended to help customers find a new perspective on commercial space and question the industry's notions around what is attractive and valuable.

> ## AUTHORLESS OBJECTS HELP CUSTOMERS QUESTION THE INDUSTRY'S NOTIONS AROUND WHAT IS ATTRACTIVE AND VALUABLE

PREVIOUS SPREAD A beautiful space, the IMMI flagship embodies a critique of normative aesthetics.

LEFT Bar lights reinforce the theme of motion in the store. Sheer panels, transparent garment racks and blood-red volumes, all in acrylic, contrast sharply with existing concrete columns, a Chinese granite floor and stainless steel carts on tracks.

ABOVE A variety of stainless steel carts roll through the store on rails embedded in the floor. The carts reference the railroads that drove the industrial age forward and the forward motion of progress and time.

Do.Do.
ŌYANE SAIKAITOKI

Form follows forebears in DO.DO.'s tribute to the local pottery trade

HASAMI — Located in Japan's Nagasaki prefecture, the town is famous for its pottery production, and Ōyane specializes in one form of the local ceramics craft: Saikai porcelain. Japanese design studio Do.Do. turned these roots into the heart and soul of the brand's new shop and gallery.

In order to channel 'the spirits of the artists' every part of the interior and exterior space is related to the local pottery tradition. The roof of the main structure resembles a classic pottery factory from the region, while Saikai porcelain is present everywhere from the toilets to the pottery shards on the steps that lead into the shop.

The location's industrial credentials are underlined by the liberal use of boshi, known in English as saggars, throughout the interior. These are ceramic crate-like containers used to protect products inside a kiln oven and have been stacked in considerable numbers to form display tables, signs and walls. Their cracked, chipped appearance forms a vivid contrast to the pristine products on display, a contrast which takes on a different form in the exterior event space, where shelving units are made of battered plastic crates and rusty pallets to confirm the impression of a modest design that forms a monumental tribute to local history.

BELOW The name Ōyane is derived from the Japanese word for large roof, and inspired the shape of the exterior event space.

FOLLOWING SPREAD Narra wood furniture provides an organic presence in the predominantly porcelain interior.

A MODEST DESIGN FORMS A MONUMENTAL TRIBUTE TO LOCAL HISTORY

Isora x Lozuraityte
Studio for Architecture

FRIENDS & FRAMES

LEFT AND ABOVE A central blue boulder represents the site's historical use as public space and city well. Made via software and the human hand, and perforated with a self-sustaining plant ecosystem, it simultaneously evokes a disappearing and emerging future.

FOLLOWING SPREAD Some design elements, like the industrial-looking floor lamps by Rafał Piesliak, were custom-made for the space by local artists, who worked within a multidisciplinary team of architects and landscape designers.

Ugnius Gelguda

ISORA X LOZURAITYTE envisions an optician's shop as the layering of past and future

VILNIUS — On a main pedestrian thoroughfare, this 151-m^2 optician and eyewear shop juxtaposes industrial aging with high-gloss, the past with the future, and the natural with the artificial. On the site of the city's earliest well and a public courtyard destroyed in World War II, the team of artists, designers and landscape architects sought to remake this public space while re-evaluating the meaning of luxury in the context of our rapidly accelerating global consumer culture.

A glassy storefront frames the original load-bearing columns of the building. Inside, the team created an atrium wrapped with a perimeter eyewear display and eliminating typical retail counter space. By exposing earlier architectural layers, they revealed a 'material language of time' that had lain, unscathed, underneath. Any surface that is not old, however, is new and reflective: from the aluminium foil-wrapped ceiling and mirrored surfaces cladding walls and mounted on large caster wheels, to the liquid lacquering of the old concrete floor under thick layers of transparent epoxy.

Artists created readymade mobile furniture for the space, including the storefront luminaires by Rafał Piesliak, a table-object by Donatas Jankauskas and curtains designed by Morta Griškevičiūtė. At the centre, a blue boulder floating above a mirrored base contains a self-sustaining plant ecosystem. The installation represents a nascent future at the heart of a fading past.

EARLIER ARCHITECTURAL LAYERS REVEAL A 'MATERIAL LANGUAGE OF TIME'

Kokaistudios
ASSEMBLE BY RÉEL

ABOVE Four themed zones transform an open 1037-m² space into an easily navigable retail environment.

Urban behavioural patterns inspire KOKAISTUDIOS' path to driving customer traffic through a men's outfitter

SHANGHAI — Assemble by Réel is a menswear store that aims to unite a variety of outspoken brands under one concept. This ethos informed the brief they passed on to Kokaistudios: translate an open 1037-m² space into one cohesive brand story. In order to do this, the Shanghai-based design outfit decided to integrate human behaviour patterns from the urban environment into the store.

'A city is comprised of points of interest where people congregate,' the designers explain. 'These anchors diffuse into avenues, streets, and lanes that form the paths that people follow naturally.' Based on these meeting points, Kokaistudios created four zones — church, park, skatepark and gallery — that act as focal points within the store.

Each has a large installation at its centre that can be seen from across the room and thus encourages the customers to keep on exploring the store. The 'church' is demarcated by archway cut-outs whose time-honoured style alludes to the classic products found here. The 'park' boasts floor-to-ceiling windows that look over Jiangan Park and a tranquil atmosphere that focuses on the more fashion-forward products found here. The 'skatepark' features an installation inspired by skate ramps that match the streetwear brands, while in the 'gallery' bright colours put the spotlight on lifestyle products, an engaging display that also serves to attract customers through the shop's secondary entrance.

THE DESIGN REINTERPRETS HUMAN
BEHAVIOUR PATTERNS FROM THE
URBAN ENVIRONMENT INTO THE STORE

LEFT A skate ramp inspired installation in the 'skates park' zone contains fitting rooms.

BELOW TOP In the Park Zone the store opens up to the outside world with large windows offering expansive views of nearby Jiangan Park.

BELOW BOTTOM The 'church' zone is characterised by arched openings.

ESSENTIALS   SKIN   BEARD   HAIR

Landini Associates
GENTSAC

LANDINI ASSOCIATES uses wood and concrete to remove stigmas surrounding male grooming stores

SYDNEY — Conventional wisdom has it that men can be reluctant shoppers at the best of times, let alone when it comes to considering cosmetics. This posed a problem for gentSac, a lifestyle product subscription service that wanted to enhance its online offering with a flagship store where men can ask for grooming advice and explore creams and potions.

Landini Associates was engaged to create a space where men will not hesitate to enter and will feel comfortable in. To do so, the Sydney-based design firm created a design that 'just like a gentleman, is cool, calm and sophisticated: more gallery space than skincare store'. At the entrance, physical barriers are removed by glass sliding doors that reveal the store's contents at a glance. The no-fuss material selection is the antithesis of a traditional cosmetics store, as concrete and timber form a functional material palette that's not quite macho, but certainly masculine.

Aside from the grooming products, the only adornments are the bags — aka gentSacs — that hang on the wall. Men can learn how best to fill these after a chat at the large consultation table in the centre of the room or a session at the testing station in the corner once they're sufficiently at ease here.

LEFT Concrete walls are offset with simple timber shelves to allow the products to be the stars of the show.

ABOVE The minimal interior aims to create a calm space that allows men to browse cosmetic products without overcomplicating things.

Landini Associates
SARAH & SEBASTIAN

LANDINI ASSOCIATES turns an empty box into a jeweller with the flick of a switch

PADDINGTON — When is a store not a store? Arguably, when there's no product. Landini Associates' design for jewellers Sarah & Sebastian is extremely minimal — at first glance it's just a glass box that appears to only have a workbench and chair inside. By stripping everything else away, the focus is put firmly on the jeweller behind the bench. Passers-by can see an artisan at work, customers see the person waiting to give them an intimate consultation.

Nonetheless, as Mark Landini, the Australian design firm's creative director, explains, there is more to the interior than meets the eye: 'There are three elements to our design. The first, is the minimalist glass box which we lined with mirrors to represent the simplicity of Sarah & Sebastian's design. The second, is the beautifully detailed timber and copper jewellers bench, an expression of their craft. The third, the alchemy of the two-way mirrors which magically unveil their treasures at the jewellers will.'

Yes, there are indeed products here after all. During a conversation on materials and process with a customer, the jeweller can flick a switch to light up sections of a one-way mirrored wall at the back of the store and reveal the collections. It's more than just a magic trick — as the jewellery is made to order, the personal nature of the transaction is more important to Sarah & Sebastian (and their customers) than showing a range of existing products.

LEFT The minimal interior creates an intimate shopping experience in which the jeweller guides each customer towards his or her perfect piece.

BELOW A mirrored wall at the back of the store conceals the jewellery collections and reflects the sandstone church across the square instead.

Ross Honeysett

Leckie Studio Architecture + Design
CHA LE MERCHANT TEAHOUSE

LECKIE STUDIO eliminates distractions to allow spiritual and sensual focus

VANCOUVER — Cha Dao is an ancient Chinese tea ceremony that stimulates health and meditation. These values are at the heart of the Cha Le Merchant Teahouse, a place where you don't just buy tea, but immerse yourself in it.

'When we spoke to the client about the reference points and ideas for this project, we proposed that the space would feel like an apothecary — a modern interpretation of a medicinal and spiritual place,' explains Michael Leckie, founder of Leckie Studio. The medicinal atmosphere is subtly set by the jars and packages of tea that line the wall of the store, recalling a classic pharmacy, but it is the spiritual side of Cha Le (Mandarin for 'happy tea') that dominates.

Just as the tea ceremony elevates humble materials into something elegant, even otherworldly, Leckie Studio took a simple material like wood and made it the teahouse's showpiece: plywood is used for the tea bar that runs nearly the length of the space. This is where the modern tea ceremony is conducted and where novices and experts alike can immerse themselves in the world of tea. By reducing the amount of distractions in a stripped, yet elegant interior, visitors' full attention can be given to the tea ceremony.

LEFT The size and quality of the tea bar was inspired by the minimal sculptures of American artist Donald Judd.

BELOW The teahouse represents a modernist interpretation of the traditional Chinese Cha Dao tea ritual.

Erna Peter

LINEHOUSE turns a store inside out by extending a curved steel display system into a textural facade

SHANGHAI — This 20-m² streetwear retail space is the second that Linehouse has designed for All Sh and it is very different from the first. The store features a curving stainless steel installation that serves two purposes: it acts as a dramatic, highly textural facade that then continues inward from the entrance to form a display system. The brushed metal panels are perforated with holes of varying dimensions in fields of diagonal rows set at different angles, creating an endlessly engaging semi-moiré across the storefront. Because the perforations make the view into the shop from the curb partly see-through, they give the window unexpected depth.

Inside, the steel panels are interrupted by niches of various sizes and shapes fitted with garment rails and shelving for the display of shoes and accessories. The designers installed T5 fluorescent tube lights into U-channels between each panel to create a strong, playful lighting effect that highlights the graphic interior. What is more, the perforations filter natural light as it enters the small space, making interior surfaces a dappled inversion of the panels. Conversely, at night light from inside the store filters onto the street in a high-contrast pattern that is more attention-grabbing than neon signage.

RIGHT The perforations in the brushed steel storefront panels — of varying size and patterns — allow light and a semi-obstructed view into the store, while also creating a textural moiré for pedestrians.

FOLLOWING SPREAD Inside, the porous panels are punctuated with niches of various sizes, containing display surfaces for accessories and garments on clothing rails.

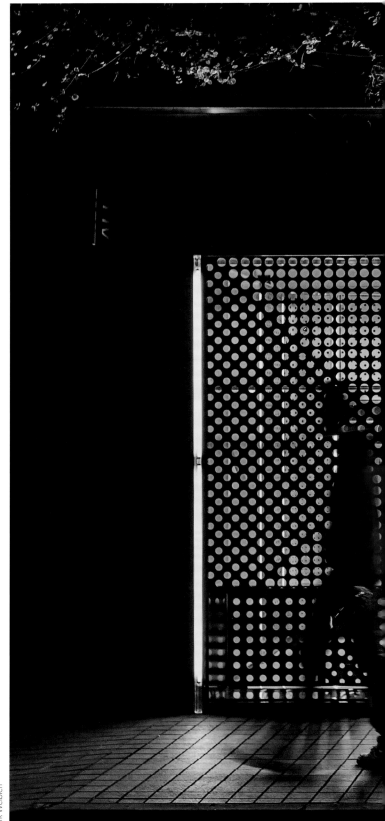

Dirk Weiblen

Linehouse
ALL SH

THE BRUSHED METAL PANELS CREATE AN ENGAGING
GRAPHIC EFFECT WHILE PROVIDING DISPLAY SOLUTIONS

THE MEDIUM IS THE MESSAGE

Marcante-Testa
IMARIKA

MARCANTE-TESTA turns an earthy, elegant architectural landscape of strong horizontals and verticals into a plush boutique

MILAN — This 180-m² women's multi-brand fashion boutique was conceived as an architectural landscape made up of earthy clay volumes and trimmed with bright copper details. The renovation and extension constructed a terrain that is carefully mapped to its function.

Panels of angular wooden screen plastered in clay organise the shop by generating various display areas for shoes, bags and accessories. Another micro-architectural element, clad in clay, serves as the fitting rooms. These elements reinforce the interior's horizontality, but find counterpoint in a system of struts assembled from copper tubing embellished with woven braid trim. The tubing supports garment rails while pointing visitors' attention toward the decorative ceiling.

Aside from bespoke lamps designed by Marcante-Testa, the rest of the lighting becomes integral to the plaster decor, transforming the ceiling into an 'upside-down carpet'. A series of large Plexiglas shelves and the globe lighting suggest a domestic setting, a milieu that the architects believe connects the clientele to the brand's products. Without interfering with the existing architectural shell, the choice of forms and materials alludes to the iconic Olivetti typewriter shops designed by Franco Albini, BBPR and other offices from the 1930s through the 1950s.

LEFT Clothes hang from or lay on transparent surfaces, like glass shelves mounted on copper struts.

FOLLOWING SPREAD LEFT Forms combining strong horizontals with intriguing verticals, as well as materials — from clay or pink briar wood to white gloss laminate, Plexiglas and copper detailing — make reference to the legendary post-war Olivetti typewriter shops.

FOLLOWING SPREAD RIGHT The furniture was designed by Marcante-Testa and realised by ODS with trim by MV1843. The velvety matte plasters covering the displays have an earthen finish that was created by Matteo Brion.

THE DESIGNERS BELIEVE A DOMESTIC SETTING ALLOWS THE CLIENTELE TO CONNECT TO THE BRAND'S PRODUCTS

Moriyuki Ochiai Architects
CRYSTALSCAPE

MORIYUKI OCHIAI crafts a sculptural beauty salon in the spirit of monodzukuri

TOKYO — As a small island country with limited resources, Japan celebrates the spirit of monodzukuri: ingenuity in the service of craftsmanship. 'From a single sheet of paper folded into a variety of shapes, emerged the art of origami,' architect Moriyuki Ochiai explains. 'From a single bolt of fabric was born one of the country's most iconic garments, the kimono, and from a single piece of cloth, used to wrap and carry objects, came the furoshiki.'

In Crystalscape, Ochiai's finite material is aluminium, which he bent and buckled into an austere planar surface that curls across the ceiling of this 110-m² salon. The luminous metal sculpture also symbolises the ideal of well-being and expresses 'the bright, aerial, gracious way' that hair cascades around the face. Its undulations evolve at seated eye-level from simple intersections of lines into a layered latticework inserted amongst planar grid objects and finished in a gradient of white to wooden tones.

The ceiling scatters diffused light as it reflects off the coiling aluminium, so that clients experience a constantly, softly shifting space. It amplifies and broadcasts changes in natural light, making them palpable throughout the day and across the seasons. That shifting light also generates variations in the purple and powdery silver tones on the walls around the shampooing area, giving the space a hushed effervescence.

Fumio Araki

LEFT The metal ribbons of the ceiling sculpture unfurl through and around the grids of the wooden latticework grids.

FOLLOWING SPREAD LEFT The aluminium waves reflect and blur the deep lavender of the painted concrete box that encloses the shampooing area, separating it from the cutting and styling section.

FOLLOWING SPREAD RIGHT In places, the architect dropped the ceiling and increased the density of the art matrix to create a more intimate space.

THE CEILING AMPLIFIES AND BROADCASTS CHANGES IN
NATURAL LIGHT, MAKING PALPABLE THE PASSAGE OF TIME

RIGI Design
MAGMODE

Arc
Atelier

COVER STORY
封面故事

———

03.

———

magmode

———

Designer Collect
Shop

RIGI DESIGN translates a multi-brand collection store into a three dimensional magazine

HUANGZHOU — Liu Kai's Shanghai-based cross-disciplinary studio designed this 600-m² multi-brand collection store to be 'a three-dimensional magazine, a readable store.' Magmode, a retailer that sells fashion and accessories of various designers, wanted RIGI to develop a unified, visually legible concept by which it could present itself as cohesive and coherent. In this bright, clearly organised space, the designers also explored a model that would represent the country's retail future.

RIGI defined various functional areas of the store as if they were the different sectors of a print magazine. In line with this concept, the shop's signature was conceived as the 'cover' of the brand, while the most recent seasonal 'content' is featured at the entrance to the store. Every display area is considered a different 'page' in the publication, presenting varying content throughout the space just as a magazine organises topics across its pages.

The editorial idea of 'publishing' regular updates is manifest in displays and signs throughout the interiors. The rear wall of the store serves as a succinct seasonal introduction of content and, every month, showcases (and sells) one book selected by a local library. Taken altogether, the store turns many into one.

PREVIOIUS SPREAD LEFT Like a magazine's table of contents and its front of book, the most recent seasonal 'content' is featured at the entrance.

PREVIOUS SPREAD RIGHT RIGI considered signage throughout the store as the 'magazine cover' of the brand in order to clarify and define a cohesive identity for Magmode.

RIGHT Every month, a local library chooses a book that is then sold along the store's back wall.

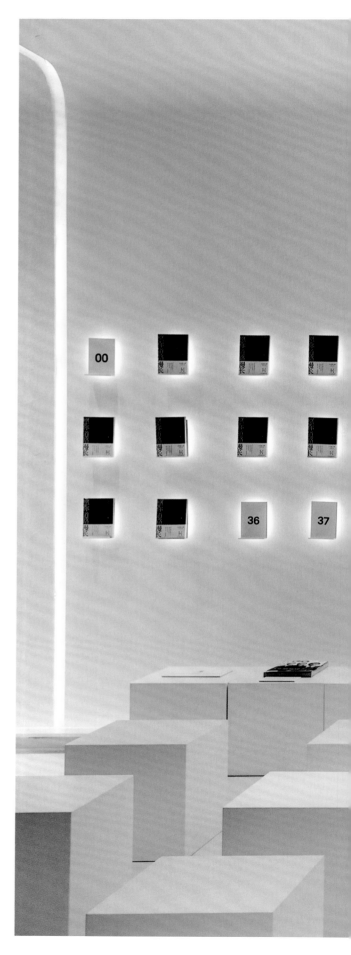

RIGI EXPLORES A SPATIAL BUSINESS MODEL THAT MAY REPRESENT RETAIL'S FUTURE

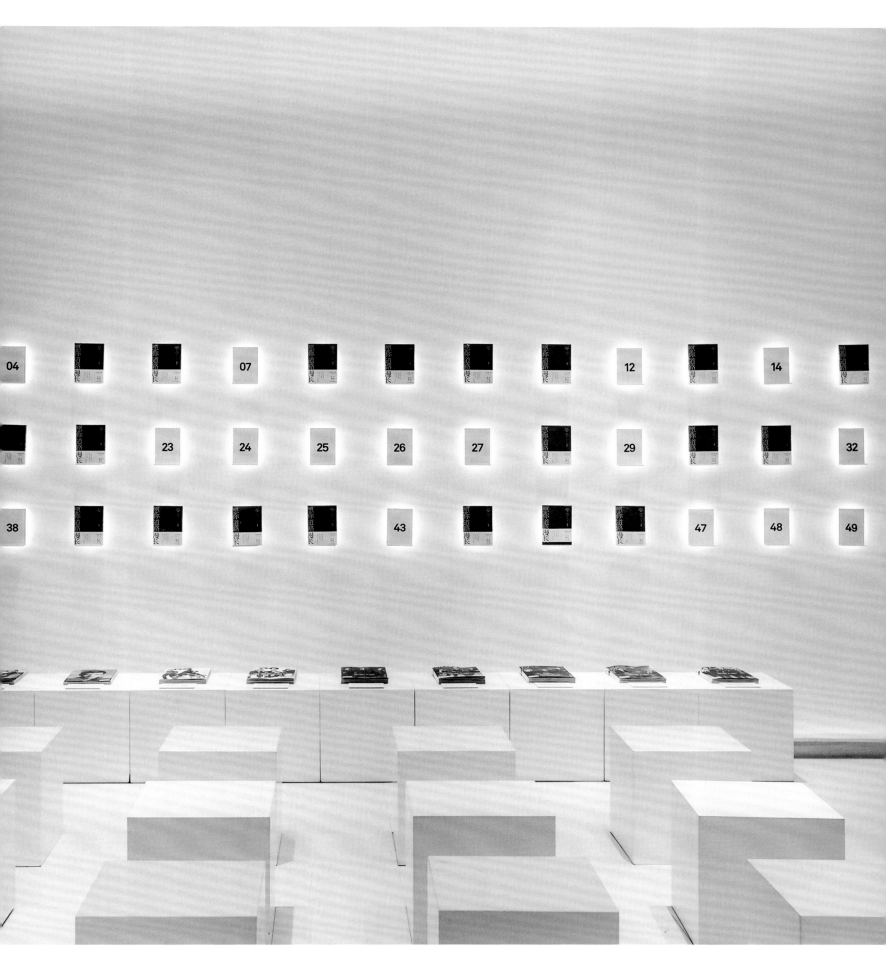

Sergio Mannino Studio
MEDLY PHARMACY

SERGIO MANNINO's playful design incorporates community into a hyper-refined environment

NEW YORK — Local patrons of Medly Pharmacy order online or from a smart phone app and get delivery to their homes within hours. Building on this digital reputation, Sergio Mannino Studio gave the brand's first physical location an unusually elegant look and feel: clean but not clinical, industrial but smooth, been-there-forever and brand new at the same time.

The goal was to turn this young business into a sell-through-every-channel retail platform where web and cash till sales work in tandem. As designers Sergio Mannino and Martina Guandalini put it, 'a successful online business needs a physical counterpart and our design for Medly has been created with this in mind.' At the same time, as a neighbourhood pharmacy, another goal was to focus on community, welcoming and connecting people.

The 176-m² space in a Brooklyn neighbourhood consists of two areas: one a cosy waiting room where customers collect prescriptions, and a larger administration space in the rear. The first features an almost completely pale aqua palette based on the brand's colour. This is expressed monolithically: through the custom-made cement counter with a green to white fading finish, white and mint green geometric tiles, and the ceiling, walls and back wall made up of corrugated metal mesh panels, all of which are rendered in the same hue.

ABOVE Green vinyl benches seat two people back-to-back like conversation chairs. These are a tribute to Shiro Kuramata, one of Japan's most important designers of the 20th century.

RIGHT The walls behind the counter are built in industrial corrugated mint green metal mesh panelling, giving the store's backdrop unexpected depth and texture.

FOLLOWING SPREAD Intimate, warm, comfortable and comforting, the interior can help connect customers to each other and to the brand.

A SUCCESSFUL ONLINE BUSINESS
NEEDS A PHYSICAL COUNTERPART

Sergio Mannino

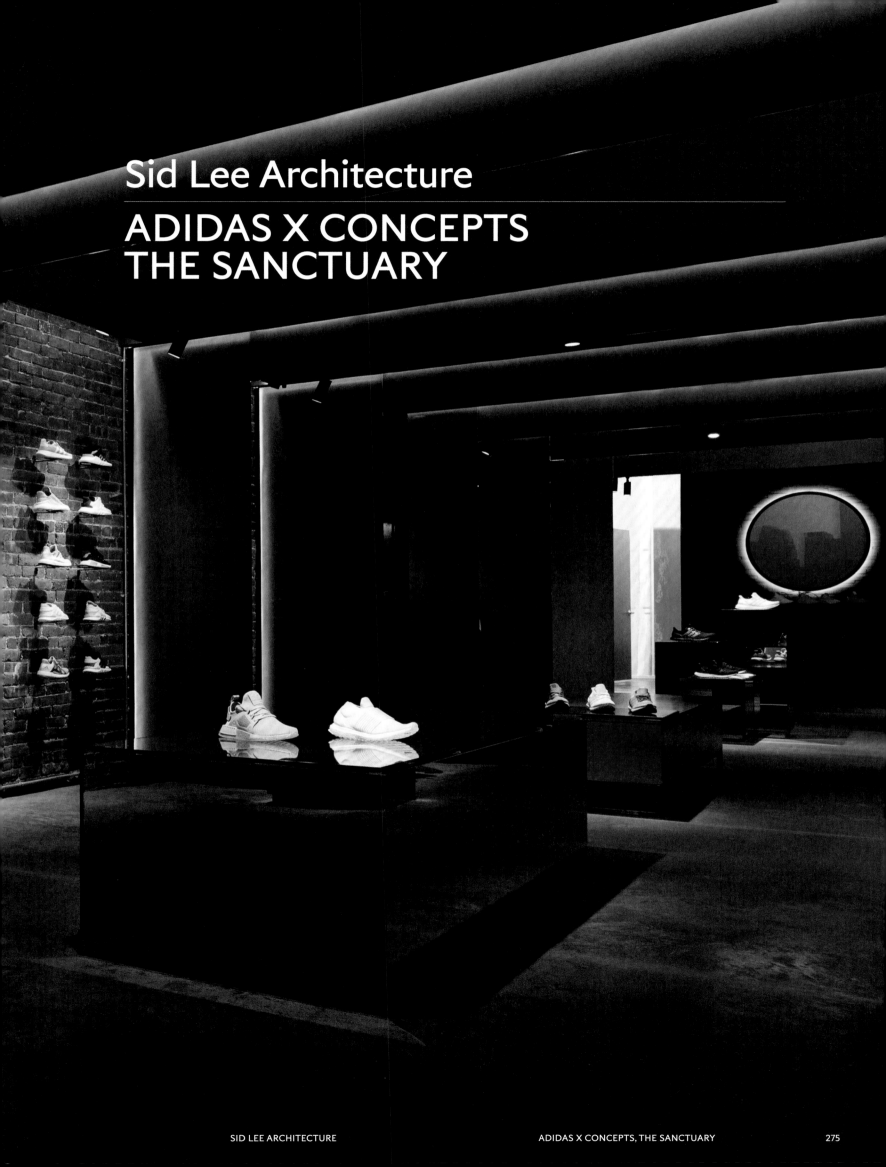

Sid Lee Architecture

ADIDAS X CONCEPTS
THE SANCTUARY

PREVIOUS SPREAD Displays make the shoes appear to float off the wall or on top of their own reflections on mirrored podiums in the middle of the room.

ABOVE Artist Jordan Söderberg Mills created shimmering boxes along the space, serving as a showcase for shoes, but also as a break-down of the light.

RIGHT Lighting and translucent glass is used to create an effect of perpetual progression within the space. A cylinder neon light podium is displayed for the wall of legends exhibition, and specially designed to drive store visits by showcasing rotating rare collections of only the rarest and most revered pairs of kicks.

SID LEE ARCHITECTURE elevates shoes to the rank of collector's item in a temple-like space

BOSTON — Montreal-based Sid Lee Architecture sanctified this urban underground to create a sacred space where sneakers have become the most coveted collectible object. The Sanctuary is a 110-m^2 showcase where the streetwear savvy and the brand faithful can gather, worship and gear up.

Like a secret, the shop is hidden in a basement on one of Boston's oldest commercial causeways and mapped with 'modular thresholds' meant to evoke feelings of discovery, pause and awe. Visitors enter via a raw steel screen door filigreed with sacred symbols (a Boston Celtics-inspired pattern) before passing through a 'field of discoveries': a choreographed series of narrowing arches that divide the room rhythmically into multiple intimate spaces, to encourage contemplation of the product. Wall perforations anchor hidden steel bracket displays that make the shoes appear to float away from the wall.

To move visitors and elicit curiosity, the designers provided surreal effects: lighting and translucent glass create the perception of constant progression through the space, while a custom glass display reflects the products in dispersed layers of colour. The Sanctuary is a liturgical space in which Concept and adidas succeeds at making materialism feel immaterial.

Studio Malka Architecture
HOMECORE CHAMPS-ELYSÉES

Laurent Clement

STUDIO MALKA turns a white space into a colour wheel that obscures spatial dimensions

PARIS — Twenty-five years ago, menswear label Homecore was the first French streetwear brand. Today, the look of the brand's newest 100-m² boutique was inspired by the iconic Krylon spray paint can and its Colour Therapy concept, which informs its fashion.

The shop is basically a 3D chromatic circle. Stéphane Malka, founder of Studio Malka, used the seven glazed arches that form the jagged facade — its five faces mean that most windows face a slightly different direction — as the starting point for his 'chromatic axis'. He mapped the angle of each window to determine at what angle to place each block of colour in silica bio paint. Against a white background, the colours spill over plinths, reclaimed wood furniture, a cash counter, walls, ceiling and floor, as if each window was stained with a single colour, casting a long late-afternoon shadow through the space.

The windows stand in for Newton's prism, which scatters white light, a synthesis of all colours, into the spectrum of discrete colours. The arching hues overlap, however, to create additive fields of colour: red overlaps blue to create purple, and yellow to create orange, for instance. The effect obscures the actual dimensions of the store, blending a wall into the floor or visually flattening the boxy volume that contains the fitting rooms. 'The project gives tangible form to the immaterial space of the spectrum,' the architect explains, 'the colour structures the space just as a material would.'

LEFT Overlapping fields of colour confuse the actual dimensions of the interior, flattening walls into ceiling and floor, or the fitting rooms into themselves.

ABOVE The crooked lines of the facade allow each window's colour to collide with others.

FOLLOWING SPREAD The shop is a 3D chromatic circle where each radiating hue corresponds to a refractive index, and each overlap of colour transforms two hues to create an additive colour.

Waterfrom Design
MOLECURE PHARMACY

PREVIOUS SPREAD Natural materials and light suffuse the space, bespeaking well-being and saluting nature. The process of 'molecular aggregation' suggested the look of the stone walls and triangular holes (molecules) are laser-cut in the stairs to create shadows that fall like leaves.

LEFT A third-generation pharmacist asked Waterfrom to subvert the stereotypical pharmacy. At the heart of the space, the trunk of a 100-year-old tree and hanging foliage surround a wooden laboratory table where pharmacists engage more fully with customers.

RIGHT The design integrates function, aesthetics and the spirit of innovation with drug display, dispensation and human interaction in the form of a spiral staircase connecting each area of the shop floor.

WATERFROM DESIGN looks to the purpose of a business to reinvent its interior

TAICHUNG — In a reification of well-being and a tribute to nature, Taipei City-based Waterfrom, looked to the object of pharmaceutics — extracting and combining certain molecules in order to synthesise curative drugs — to develop the design concept of this 120-m² pharmacy.

A two-floor copper spiral staircase, recalling the double helix of a DNA strand, was installed as a way to link the three types of transaction occurring at Molecure: drug display, experimentation with dispensing methods and human interactions that foster well-being. The fact that making drugs involves 'molecular aggregation' inspired the designers to clad the pharmacy's double-height walls with cobblestones and cement, creating a rough texture that lends a sense of solid reality to an almost ethereal space.

What is more, the designers avoided the typical pharmacy counter, where service flows in one direction, by making the heart of the space a laboratory table where pharmacists can engage more fully with customers. Together with the open dispensing area and an iPad-integrated consulting service, an unusual degree of human interaction takes place in a light and air-filled space, re-framing the pharmacy experience as one that is about healing instead of illness.

> A LIGHT AND AIR-FILLED SOCIAL SPACE RE-FRAMES THE PHARMACY EXPERIENCE AS ONE THAT IS ABOUT HEALING INSTEAD OF ILLNESS

Yagyug Douguten
BAKE CHEESE TART

With local history and galvanized steel YAGYUG DOUGUTEN builds a temple to industrial labour and the cheese tart

OSAKA — In an underground oblong corner space, this 25-m² cheese tart bakery offers out-of-the-oven freshness while putting the production process on display. Nara-based Fumitaka Suzuki of studio Yagyug Douguten activates multiple senses by evoking the heat, sizzle and scent of freshly made cheese tarts through the use of galvanized steel furnishings whose chromate-treated surfaces have a yellow, gold and rainbow burnish. The contrast between the tarts' soft creaminess and the industrial plating becomes a visual analogue of the sizzle of dough placed in a baking tray.

In the bustling market hall setting of a department store, instead of 'shouting' to gain attention, Suzuki wrapped the bakery in a glass curtain wall with rounded corners. The glass sets it apart from its surroundings, giving it a temple-like aura of hushed calm. In fact, the designer was inspired, in part, by a Buddha statue in the city's Shitennoji Temple. This area of Osaka was once home to both historic temples and galvanization factories that supported the ascendance of Japan's post-war economy. A retail space that honours the city's physical and spiritual labours generates a contrast that Suzuki hopes will feed visitors' interest in the place as much as the product.

PREVIOUS SPREAD In the noisy food hall of a department store, Suzuki engages passers-by by wrapping a temple-like quiet around the golden bakery in the form of a glass curtain wall. Customers are served through a pastille-shaped hole in the glass.

BELOW Each steel-clad fixture has a clear function based on production. Detailed studies helped build each tool and stage in the process — from baking, storage and display to cooling, customer service, packaging and a fire door — into the main pillar.

RIGHT 'I must admit my imprudence,' Suzuki says. 'My inspiration was, in part, the fact that a galvanized Buddha statue looked "delicious" in my eyes.'

Zentralnorden
SPOONING

Patrick Nitzsche

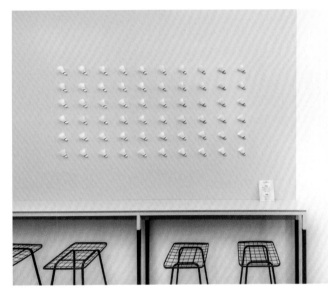

ZENTRALNORDEN'S colourful, graphical cookie dough bar is as grown-up as it is playful

BERLIN - 'Colour, colour, colour' is key to a soothingly rosy 22-m^2 bar designed by local studio Zentralnorden for German brand Spooning. On a budget as small as the shop, the designers transformed a narrow, dim storefront into a simple, cheerful space. The centrepiece is a 3-m-high freestanding counter where ten different types of cookie dough and toppings are on offer and an attention-grabbing yellow handle allows small children to step up to countertop level to eyeball the batter-filled bowls.

But the bar isn't just for kids. The colour palette — pink walls, yellow detailing, white tiles and navy blue steel bar stools by Isimar Faro — is meant to put visitors of any age in a contented, licking-the-mixing-bowl-clean state of mind.

The team's background in graphic design is also evident in the space's wall art: a grid of badminton shuttlecocks and a menu board consisting of large individual letters hand-stamped on plywood. The lighting — ordinary LED tubes ranged further apart in the front of the bar and closer in the back — gives the space greater visual depth while drawing customers inside. In order to tap into social media branding opportunities, a humorous neon sign reads: '#forgetyourdiet'.

LEFT Colour choices reinforce the graphic look of this cookie dough bar: kid-friendly yellow handles help little ones reach the self-service bar, white tiles create a soft grid and LED tubes add depth to the room.

ABOVE RIGHT Also adding to the graphic look is an artful shuttlecock installation that lends texture. On the opposite wall, plywood letter blocks spell out the daily menu across rows of shallow pink shelves.

THIS IS NOT JUST A CONSUMER GOOD

RETAIL SPACE AS A GALLERY

Interview
JOHANNES TORPE

Danish designer JOHANNES TORPE highlights the importance of valuing authenticity over tendencies when it comes to creating efficient brand experiences and ensuring the overall success of a brand.

What are the key factors at play in your work in retail design? I think with modern technology the demand of creating an experience within retail is more and more important. We have to give customers a reason to go into a store instead of buying online, so our approach will always be to look at what is the best practice for the client we are helping: what their outreach is, where their markets are strongest and where they can differentiate themselves from their competitors.

What about the main challenges? We cannot help anyone unless they are willing to make the necessary changes. This can sometimes include going back to the root of the brand's DNA to make sure that the direction is right and that there is a deeper understanding of their past and present to enable us to gain a better perspective of their future.

This year your design for United Cycling (p.340) won the Frame Award for Multi-brand Store of the Year. The design was praised for letting the product remain the hero. How do you achieve a distinctive retail interior without obfuscating the product? It obviously depends on the product you sell. In the case of United Cycling, we made some hard-core choices by treating the product as the god of our cycling cathedral and leaving it up to the customer to decide how to interact with both the product and the space. I do believe that this approach has made the space absolutely wonderful to experience, and it has also given the products the ability to shine above all.

What do you think ensures the success of a store? In the past I would say location, but United Cycling, in the small village of Lynge in Denmark, has proven that experience is more important. In that location, 60 per cent of the customers leave with a purchase and in its one year of operation the traffic continues to increase, with people coming a long way for the experience.

Establishing flagship store locations on every street corner of the world's metropolitan cities is no longer single-handedly the recipe for success. If they want to catch the attention of the new generation of consumers, luxury brands need to become a whole lot smarter in delivering their DNA in a much more experience-based direction. It is simply not enough to be a famous name...

What impact do you think factors like online shopping and 'the age of the influencer' have had in retail design? Influencers are for sure future advertising tools, but if you create your brand only to satisfy them, you will be compromising the integrity of your product for something that is based on tendencies and movements of big data. The moment a brand replaces authenticity with tendencies, it is on a short-sighted and dangerous road to self-destruction.

To design responsibly, we need to be more focused on creating real, tactile experiences that will let customers connect emotionally with the product by feeling, smelling, and almost 'tasting' what it can give them.

How do you envision the future of retail design? You can never predict the future, but we can hope that the human connection will remain the focus and the experience will remain the goal.

'THE MOMENT A BRAND REPLACES AUTHENTICITY WITH TENDENCIES, IT IS ON A SHORT-SIGHTED AND DANGEROUS ROAD TO SELF-DESTRUCTION'

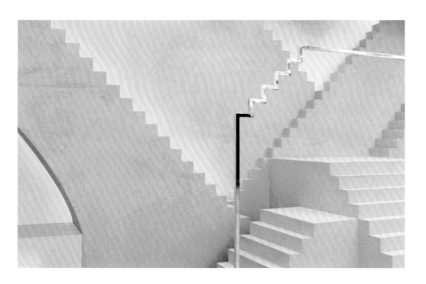

ANAGRAMA's interior concept encourages a fashion boutique to embrace its eccentricity

SAN PEDRO — Multidisciplinary creative agency Anagrama has been a part of the history of fashion boutique Novelty since its very beginnings, having been responsible for its graphic identity and first store design. In 2016, the Mexican studio was asked to further develop the brand, which features quirky, handpicked items from New York, by creating a space where visitors can enjoy the experience of buying high fashion clothing and accessories.

To do this, the team designed an interior that feels more like an art installation than a shop, by filling the store with an excess of staircases, some of which can be used, others that are purely decorative. Inside, customers are transported into a world reminiscent of M C Escher's illustrations, where up is down and down is up.

A further play on perspective is provided by the placement of lighting in alcoves and recesses, adding extra shadows and depth. Marble slabs and tables offer a return to solid ground while subtly alluding to the luxury of what is on display. To ensure that the store keeps its femininity, the walls are decorated simply in pink plaster. A finish that, just like Novelty itself, is warm, rugged and ever so slightly eccentric.

ABOVE Slabs of marble underscore the luxurious nature of the fashion products that the brand offers its customers.

RIGHT Rugged plaster walls have been painted in a pink pastel colour to create a warm yet edgy atmosphere.

FOLLOWING SPREAD The geometric lines of the staircases are accentuated by a play of light and shadows.

Estudio Tampiquito

Anagrama
NOVELTY

POWERSHOP 6

THIS IS NOT JUST A CONSUMER GOOD

CUSTOMERS ARE
TRANSPORTED INTO A WORLD
REMINISCENT OF M C ESCHER'S
ILLUSTRATIONS, WHERE UP IS
DOWN AND DOWN IS UP

THIS IS NOT JUST A CONSUMER GOOD

Brinkworth
BROWNS EAST

Ed Reeve

A FAMILY OF SCULPTURAL 3D COLLAGES SERVE AS DISPLAY FURNISHINGS

BRINKWORTH prototypes an omni-channel retail blueprint that is as elegant and eclectic as the fashion for sale

LONDON — In its first new retail location in 20 years, a refined but Memphis-inspired mix of materials suits the eclectic aesthetic of luxury multi-brand retailer Browns Fashions. The 480-m² space collages colours, textures and forms in the same spirit as the label's glossy burgundy coats with yellow faux fur trim and its rainbow-patterned puffers or its chemises, armoured with sequins in a violet to red shading.

In a concept shop format combining fashion with art and furniture, Brinkworth blended physical shopping and e-commerce. The store will also serve as a template for Browns Nomadic projects, a series of roaming, semi-permanent retail destinations.

The open-plan space consists of a family of sculptural 3D collages that serve as mid-floor, interchangeable display furnishings fabricated from metal sheet in copper, stainless steel and green mirrored steel, as well as timber veneers, acrylics and lacquers, with plinths in Corian, timber, cork and recycled Smile and Durat plastics. The ground-floor fixtures emphasise geometric forms — arches, spheres, hemispheres, intersecting planes — and surface layers that range from metallic to matte, opaque to sheer, solid to iridescent. Embracing a synthetic aesthetic, the designers used artificial materials in a way that looks as natural as the salvaged timber floors and fur walls of the cylindrical changing rooms.

BRINKWORTH translates a refined, sculptural retail concept into a semi-permanent 'nomadic' boutique

LOS ANGELES — Based on a 'blueprint' retail concept designed by Brinkworth for the London-based label Browns Fashions (featured on page 300 of this book), the brand's store-in-store pop-up on Sunset Blvd presents its first foray outside the UK.

On a tight deadline, the studio designed and produced an interior concept intended to have an 8-week lifespan. The temporary space, located at Fred Segal's, clearly referenced the London store's colour scheme and textures, which itself was a strong expression of the diversity of the multi-brand retailer's product offerings — furniture, fashion, accessories and art — and their exuberant materiality.

Reflecting the brand's embrace of the synthetic as much as the organic, the classical as much as the progressive, the LA interior further amplified its already diverse family of materials, from sumptuous marble slabs to eminently utilitarian packaging materials. For example, panels of shiny laminate and recycled plastics and bolts of metallic bubble wrap sheeting, were placed in customised (and easily portable) industrial trolleys in order to create a scenography impromptu-looking combinations of backdrops and displays that could be reconfigured in minutes.

Erik Melvin

Brinkworth
BROWNS LA POP-UP

SEEMINGLY IMPROMPTU COMBINATIONS OF BACKDROPS AND DISPLAYS CAN BE RECONFIGURED IN MINUTES

PREVIOUS SPREAD The storefront, like a Memphis movement collage, showcased the diverse materiality of the new Browns retail concept – the combination proving both eclectic and elegant. The result reflected the ranging playfulness and complementary contrasts of the multi-brand retailer's products.

LEFT Perhaps the most elegant of the utilitarian materials were the long cardboard tubes used to build cylindrical fitting rooms.

RIGHT AND BELOW Sheets of material were set upright into bespoke industrial trolleys to create displays. These set lush marble slab beside utilitarian materials, making recycled post-industrial plastic and silver bubble wrap feel luxurious.

Burdifilek
MOOSE KNUCKLES

Ben Rahn, A-Frame Studio

Creativity and commerce collide in a cabinet of curiosities carefully curated by BURDIFILEK

TORONTO — Although Moose Knuckles was keen to make the transition from wholesale to retail, the Canadian outerwear brand wanted its first flagship store to retain an air of independence. Therefore, Burdifilek was asked to create a space that would engage with customers beyond sales transactions. The local design firm's response was an edgy interior serving as a cabinet of curiosities that customers have to explore to find the products.

The quest begins at the entrance, where a 3D extraction of the brand logo splits the storefront in three to offer a tantalising glimpse of the products inside whilst obscuring the sales point and changing rooms. Contrasts and paradoxes continue inside, where creativity and commerce seamlessly blend into one another. Products are the centre of attention, but culture is strongly represented by hanging televisions that stream curated video art.

A happy medium between luxurious and rugged materials represents the brand's role as a supplier of warm products for cold weather. High-resin mirrors, polished stainless steel and a glowing white wall represent the cold, set against an end-cut black locust block for a dynamic contrast. Warmth is supplied by the winter jackets and the leather straps and fur wrapping that adorn the store's centrepiece: a floating raceway upon which the collection hangs.

ABOVE Limited edition products are exhibited in mirrored cabinets of curiosities that await the customers.

RIGHT The silhouette of an exposed stockroom adds a level of intrigue to the store that invites customers to explore forbidden territory.

FOLLOWING SPREAD By placing limited edition products in glass cabinets and wrapping the floating raceway in fur, Burdifilek aims to contrast manufactured design with raw natural beauty.

THE BALANCE BETWEEN
LUXURY AND RUGGEDNESS
REPRESENTS THE BRAND'S
ROLE AS A SUPPLIER OF
COLD WEATHER GEAR

antoniolupi

Calvi Brambilla
ANTONIOLUPI

CALVI BRAMBILLA uses the architecture of the ceiling to explore novel means of representation of domestic spaces

MILAN — With 14 large windows facing the street, Antoniolupi's showroom in Porta Tenaglia is eminently open to the city. From outside, the narrow 550-m² space resembles a glassed-in arcade where daily living is about to unfold before one's eyes. Indeed, local architects Calvi Brambilla made the space a stage set, containing a series of bath furniture vignettes.

With an emphasis on well-being, the architects were inspired by the vaults and domes of traditional Turkish baths. In particular, Kılıç Ali Paşa designed in the 1570s by Ottoman architect and engineer Mimar Sinan. Here, the lower portions of the room, at the level of the human eye, contain the baths and fountains while far overhead light perforates its large domes. Thus, the architects decided to focus primarily on the showroom's ceiling, which consists of purposefully irregular vaults that do not always align with the window openings. This strategy allowed them to keep the floor free of structural obstacles that might have hindered its future reconfigurations. As a backdrop to the white vaulting, visible through the storefront, a matte black rear wall of coarse plaster gives the scenography both depth and contrast.

LEFT The entrance to the showroom looks more like that of a luxury fashion house.

FOLLOWING SPREAD The vaults leave the floor open to rapid and total re-staging of the collections. The floor is an irregular stone composite common to Milanese architecture called Ceppo di Gré.

CLOU architects
JIUXI WEDDING EXHIBITION

 THIS IS NOT JUST A CONSUMER GOOD

Shuhe

CLOU ARCHITECTS embraces technology to bring a bridal boutique into the 21ˢᵗ century

BEIJING — Think of any bridal shop and any number of images might flow into your mind, most of which probably involve white, pink and frills. Beijing wedding planners Jiuxi, however, wanted to leave these clichés behind in favour of embracing a contemporary environment that showed off the full range of their services. There's no escaping the bridal gowns in CLOU architects' concept (nor should there be), but neon lights and black anodized steel cladding create an almost surgical atmosphere that alerts customers to the brand's modern approach to wedding planning within what the designers describe as 'a sleek, highly organised jewellery box with modern digital influences'.

Everything in the interior works to provide couples and their families with the best possible vision of their big day and the days after: instead of merely pulling out brochures, couples are invited to ascend an interactive honeymoon exhibition hosted on a central rotunda. This features 360-degree LED projection screens and VR headsets that couples can use to experience any and every aspect of their personalised wedding package, including dream honeymoon destinations. To prove that technology is compatible with romance, a selection of classic romantic movie scenes are displayed on screens spread throughout the boutique.

LEFT Even in a futuristic design concept, bridal gowns still dominate the wedding planning shop interior.

FOLLOWING SPREAD RIGHT TOP Large dividing mirrors break up the large floor area and allow brides the best possible view of themselves in their potential outfits.

FOLLOWING SPREAD RIGHT BOTTOM Digital technology and VR headsets enable couples to visualise their big day on screens, not just in their minds.

EVERYTHING IN THE
INTERIOR WORKS TO
PROVIDE CUSTOMERS
WITH THE BEST POSSIBLE
VISION OF THEIR BIG DAY

Curiosity

DOLCE & GABBANA

Alessandra Chemollo

LEFT AND ABOVE The glass facade spans two storeys and its curtain-like appearance invites passers-by to take a peek behind it.

FOLLOWING SPREAD Classical art is supported by luxurious materials in a theatrical interior that doesn't hold back on the drama.

CURIOSITY brings Milan to Miami to stage a classic Italian drama

MIAMI — This wasn't Curiosity's first project for Dolce & Gabbana, and the brief remained the same as the others: 'surprise me'. For the Italian fashion icon's Miami store, the Japanese studio decided to combine the sun of Miami and the stateliness of Milan's La Scala theatre — one of D&G's favourite buildings — to go 'behind the curtain'.

The curtain, in this instance, is a two-storey glass facade that uses wavy surfaces and the Florida sun to make it look as if the material is rippling. In doing so, it sets the tone for an inviting theatrical event. Once on the other side, visitors are transported into a spectacular interior where the line between backstage and centre stage is blurred. Are the classic Italian sculptures performers or props? Or is the collection the real star of the show?

Used liberally throughout the store, Italian travertine could also claim a headline role, supported ably in its quest for luxury by a large baroque mirror and walnut furniture with polished steel and gold velvet fittings. The only place in which you can really be sure what's what is upstairs, where the exposed ceiling reveals the lighting rigs, a clear nod to a theatre's backstage area.

POWERSHOP 6 THIS IS NOT JUST A CONSUMER GOOD

Diogo Aguiar Studio and Andreia Garcia Architectural Affairs

PRUDÊNCIO STUDIO

DIOGO AGUIAR AND ANDREIA GARCIA create a store that is minimal, movable, flexible, reflective and futuristic

PORTO — This 76-m² concept shop for Senhor Prudêncio, the urban streetwear label of designer João Pedro Filipe, was a collaboration between two local architecture studios. Filipe's forthright fashions plumb myriad aspects of city culture; he wanted the shop to do the same. 'We wanted to create a space — void of ornamentation and colour — that could emphasise Prudêncio's designs by exhibiting them in a minimal futuristic space, the universe that we believe they come from,' say the architects.

Because the existing interior was limited, they developed a solution that could double-task as a way to 'stretch' the space by increasing the perception of its length while serving as a convertible system that could be reconfigured into multiple scenarios. On the floor, they designed three lines of reflective movable vertical panels that can be moved into various compositions with four lines of white light overhead, and galvanized metal furniture for display. Aguiar and Garcia constructed the suspended panels themselves, from inexpensive thermal insulation screens, creating a space that feels simultaneously metallic and textile.

Materially, the design focuses on the reflective qualities of the furniture frames and thermal insulation screen. They used these to establish a futuristic minimalist space that is nonetheless highly tactile, reinforcing that character through the slender luminaires of cold white light overhead.

RIGHT The thermal panels seem as pliable as a textile and as hard as metal, while imbuing the space with a futuristic quality.

FOLLOWING SPREAD LEFT The railroad interior, with simple linoleum floor and bright white walls, is defined by elements of rigid linearity and layering that emphasise its narrow depth.

FOLLOWING SPREAD RIGHT The galvanized metal display furnishings have the shape of extruded rectangular outlines, echoing the thinner rectangles of lights above, both of which reinforce the perception that the space is deeper than it actually is.

 THIS IS NOT JUST A CONSUMER GOOD

Eduard Eremchuk
GUAPA FLOWER SHOP

EDUARD EREMCHUK composes a luminous white box gallery to frame flowers as works of art

ROSTOV-ON-DON — On the ground floor of a constructivist building designed in 1928 by Michail Kondratyev, there is a flower shop that represents a framing of Soviet history within a new generation of Russian architectural design, and vice-versa.

While preserving and showcasing elements of the existing building, starting with its gnarled old walls, Eremchuk turned its back on the tropes of the conventional flower shop interior: salvaged wood, dark cosy colours, potted plants and warm lighting. 'When we designed this store, we weren't thinking about a flower shop,' says Eremchuk. 'We understood that flowers are an art, themselves, and that we just needed to maintain their natural beauty.' So they created a gallery where the flowers are the art.

With a low ceiling and only one window, the designer turned the floor into an abstracted, monochrome garden. The entire ceiling, in a nod to Stanley Kubrick's 2001: A Space Odyssey, became a soft, synthetic afternoon sky through the use of a seamless vinyl film that conceals diode lights above it. In the main room, Eremchuk designed a 4-m-long work table made, like the cash desk and other furnishings, of stainless steel. The retail floor at the front is separated from the private space in the rear, where refrigerated storage for the flowers is located, by a silver volume.

PREVIOUS SPREAD The white box interior, with white Forbo vinyl flooring, echoes that of contemporary art galleries without distracting from the shape, colour, texture and fragrance of the flowers.

ABOVE Located on the ground floor of a Constructivist building, the avant-garde interior design of this florist lives side-by-side with Soviet architectural history.

RIGHT A small stainless steel bench offers a place for visitors to wait while bouquets are made up. Steel furniture was designed by Eremchuk and manufactured locally.

Eduard Eremchuk
LIKESHOP

Inna Kablukov

LEFT Inspired by the Asian trend to make commercial spaces that resemble cultural spaces, Eremchuk painted one room white like a gallery and placed a sculptural fitting room at the centre, like an artwork on show.

ABOVE The furniture, from the table and chair in the ante-room to the garment racks and coloured glass plinths on the main retail floor were custom-made. The designer used the brand's own wild colour palette, echoing the youthful exuberance of its fashion.

FOLLOWING SPREAD The ante-room antic-ipates the gallery-like retail floor beyond by its resemblance to an artwork, namely, a light installation by James Turrell, which inspired it.

Furry pink walls help EDUARD EREMCHUK bring the fitting room to centre stage

ROSTOV-ON-DON — To create this invigoratingly colourful 46-m^2 boutique, Eremchuk applied the lo-cal fashion label's own signature colour scheme — as wild and cacophonous as its clothes — to the interi-ors, making any experience in it memorable and self-consciously instagrammable.

He began by painting all the surfaces of the first reception room and office, including the furniture, entirely yellow. A mirror covering one wall reflects the yellow box back at itself, recalling a light installa-tion by James Turrell. But Eremchuk was also inspired by the Asian trend of making museum or gallery-like shop interiors. In contrast with the yellow ante-room, the main retail space is as plain white as a white box gallery. At its centre, not to one side or in an out-of-the-way corner, he placed the stand-alone box of the fitting room, as if it were an art object. Inspired by Alexander McQueen's petal gowns, he then clad the box in neon pink faux-fur shag. 'Usually the fitting room is a utilitarian space,' Eremchuk says, 'but we decided to make it part of an exhibition space.' Colourful details — visible to passers-by on the street — enliven the room: glass display podiums that stand at various heights and iridescent mirrors that rest against the walls on the Forbo vinyl floor.

THE DESIGN WAS INSPIRED BY THE ASIAN TREND
OF MUSEUM OR GALLERY-LIKE SHOP INTERIORS

Ito Masaru Design Project / SEI
ISAMU KATAYAMA BACKLASH

ITO MASARU consecrates the cycle of creation and destruction in a boutique that feels like hallowed ground

BEIJING — 'Life and death, demise and vigour,' says Ito Masaru, describing the interiors of his Chinese flagship for Isamu Katayama Backlash. It is a spot-on description of this unusual boutique, a space in which 'ruins and paradise co-exist'.

Backlash eschews the mass market, handcrafting leather garments and accessories using experimental techniques. Having designed the brand's first Tokyo flagship, Masaru followed up with this 92-m² shop inside a windowless bunker-like room. An interior wall divides it into two flanking spaces: on one side, a lounge and cash desk; on the other, the fashion. A large cross cut from one section of the wall offers intriguing glimpses of the room beyond, but this section can also pivot open, like a turnstile, to create two passages between rooms.

Facing mirrored walls in the second room infinitely reflect and exaggerate the dimensions of the dim space. On the right, limited-edition Backlash products are stored in eight large, wall-mounted, back-lit lockers, suspended above the floor and painted to look distressed with age. On the left, a living wall of dazzling green plants thrives behind glass. While the lockers recall hulking ruins, the greenery and glass proclaim the opposite. By juxtaposing the rough, old and austere with the new and unblemished, Masaru has imagined an almost sacred space that radiates strength and renewal.

PREVIOUS SPREAD A pivoting section of the interior wall is a door that allows visitors to pass from one room to the next. A cross-shape cut through it has become a signature of the brand.

ABOVE Two facing walls of mirror reflect a row of eight monolithic lockers into infinity.

Johannes Torpe Studios
UNITED CYCLING

RIGHT The space also includes a bike-fitting area, meeting rooms, a storage facility and an outdoor plaza that can be used for industry gatherings and events with the exterior clad in perforated white lacquered aluminium plates, concrete tiles and wooden lamellas.

FOLLOWING SPREAD Displays were all purpose-built and offer a variety of ways to showcase the bikes and accessories while keeping the retail floor clear and easy to navigate.

JOHANNES TORPE anoints a modern-day monastery devoted to the science of cycling

LYNGE — The client asked that this 1650-m^2 bicycle showroom be built as a Nordic hub for cycling. The project also includes ancillary spaces for staff and other facilities. The goal was to create a futuristic retail experience, a showroom that surpasses the traditional functions of retail and inspires people to dream. In short, the idea was to create the modern monastery for the science of cycling. Hence, all the functions of the facility may be transferred to those of a monastery: the product gallery is the library, the showroom is the chapel and the workshop is the forge.

Visually, however, the interiors were modelled on the detailed engineering of a carbon fibre bicycle and feature materials such as raw and black steel, ultra-clear and reflective glass, aluminium, linoleum and back-lighting. Some thresholds and certain walls were made in oak and have a more organic feel. Thus, through materials, the space celebrates cycling's contradictions — science and nature, man and machine, engineering and emotion. Torpe's team achieved this by juxtaposing visual elements that communicate these dualities.

Then, keeping the showroom floor uncluttered and sightlines clear, they floated the bikes in various ways throughout the space, displaying them inside geometric frames, in wall niches, from the ceiling, against walls — anywhere but on the floor.

junya.ishigami+associates
JINS

A minimal interior is designed for maximum efficiency by JUNYA ISHIGAMI

SHANGHAI — As an architect, perhaps it was unsurprising that Junya Ishigami's goal for this project was to create a work of architecture indoors. Nonetheless, it was the location of the Jins store in the Shanghai World Financial Centre that drove Ishigami to create a 'huge emptiness within the crowded shopping mall'. Almost everything, including colour, was stripped away in a minimal interior where form follows function.

Five monolithic 12-m-long and 25-cm-deep concrete blocks dominate the store and, despite their volume, seem to float in the air. While three display eyewear products, the other two are used for customer assistance and product assembly. Each contains a pre-stressed steel cantilever structure covered with tons of concrete positioned at the same height of 80 cm to create a low, flat landscape. The dimensions and volume aren't merely eye candy: the length, width and depth have been carefully considered to ensure the maximum linear display and enable easy circulation for customers.

Ishigami's concept is so minimal that there isn't even a storefront. All that separates the store from the corridor are solid steel shutters. Once these rise, the line between corridor and store blurs, so much so that customers wishing to move between the concrete blocks must leave the store to re-enter it.

PREVIOUS SPREAD The vast volumes of the concrete blocks enable a huge array of product stock to be displayed.

BELOW Exposed piping forms a stark contrast to the polished elegance of the eyewear products beneath.

RIGHT Tables extend right to the edge of the store premises, meaning that customers have to leave the store to enter another aisle.

THIS IS NOT JUST A CONSUMER GOOD

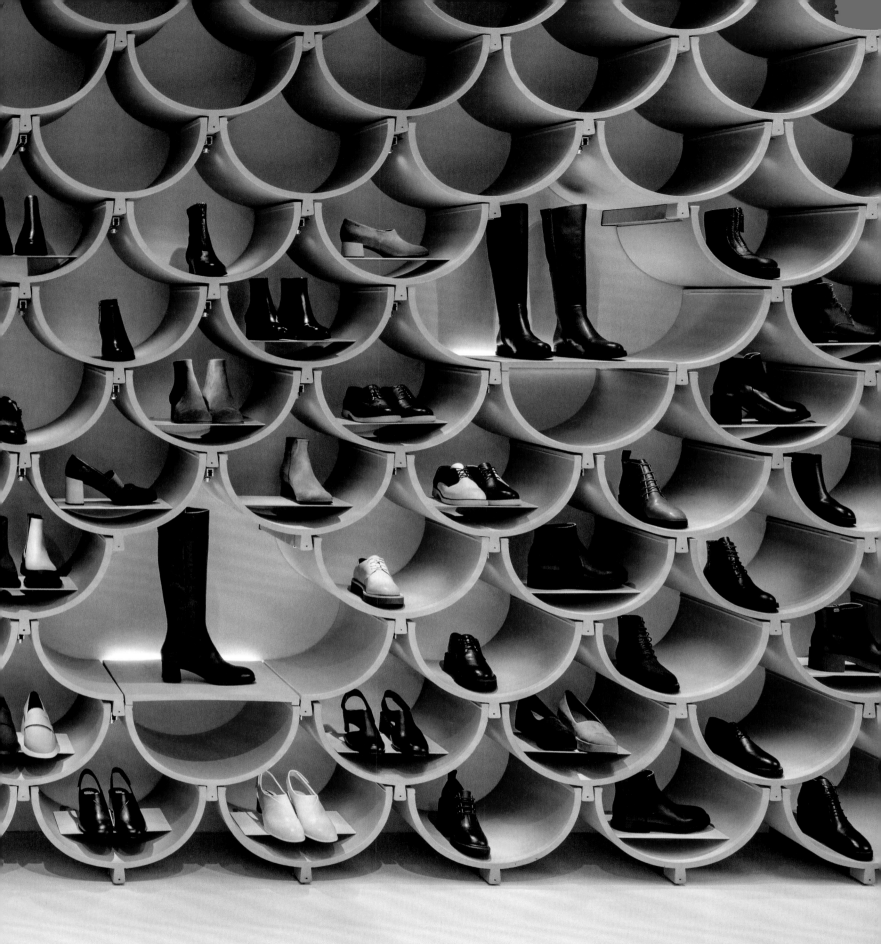

Kengo Kuma & Associates
CAMPER

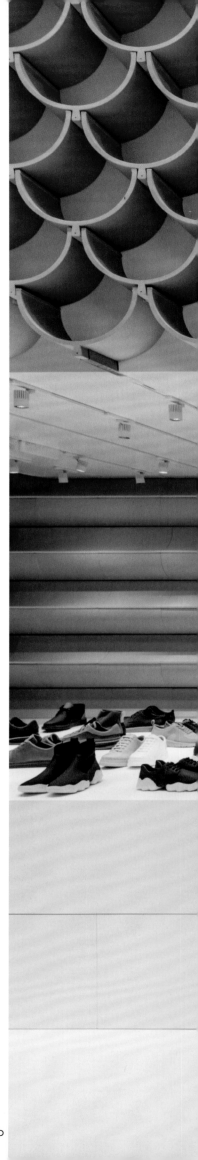

Through repetition, KENGO KUMA makes an entire shoe store from a single humble tile

BARCELONA — In this shoe store facing the Plaza Catalonia, the architects wanted to display each item separately in order to bring more attention to individual products. This suggested a niche display system, which Kengo Kuma & Associates decided to construct with vaulted ceramic plates usually used for the form-work of floor slabs, a method that replaced wooden beams and was pioneered in Catalonia.

Both Japan and Spain have a long tradition of using architectural tiles, but each culture crafts the tile in a distinct way: roof tiles in Japan are glazed and shiny while those in the Mediterranean are left bare, exposing their natural texture.

Even though their shape is very simple, by linking and repeating these ceramic elements, the team was able to generate texture and complexity throughout the space, while creating niches for each product, and solving every display requirement. These rudimentary elements became the basic, modular unit of walls, shelves, display surfaces, the cash counter and even a bench for weary shoppers. 'It is exciting for us to use such an old traditional material and find new ways to craft it, shape it, and combine its units, creating different architectural elements that can solve the needs of contemporary life,' says Kuma.

PREVIOUS SPREAD The tiles give the store pattern, texture and complexity in addition to furniture and displays.

RIGHT Always looking for alternate materials to replace concrete and steel, the designers wanted to explore the difference between Japanese and Mediterranean tile craft and ended up building walls, benches, display niches and tables by simply linking basic units of tile.

Arjen Schmitz

POWERSHOP 6

THIS IS NOT JUST A CONSUMER GOOD

Maurice Mentjens
KIKI'S STOCKSALE

MAURICE MENTJENS proves that less is more in giving an outlet store a premium update

MAASTRICHT — Kiki's Stocksale is an outlet store for Kiki Niesten Maastricht, an avant-garde fashion boutique. As such, its design needed to reflect the quality of the premium brands it stocks as well as a wish for 'a light, open, and clearly-organised presentation space that could be completed relatively quickly.' Already familiar with the location after creating the original interior in 2006, Maurice Mentjens decided to update it by stripping the narrow, high-ceilinged 16th-century location down to the bare essentials: an empty white room whose only adornments are fixtures that make the most of the long, narrow dimensions.

Recessed architectural elements in the form of stairs and supporting columns restrict the available space, but these were countered by placing clothing racks between the columns. The racks are made of black steel and floor-to-ceiling scaffolding tubes which, in combination with the overhead light fixtures, form a series of parallel lines that guide visitors through the shop. Another flexible solution was to turn the walls into displays by fitting them with white steel discs that can be used to showcase items with the help of magnets.

The monochrome design throws the focus on the colourful polka dots that adorn the linoleum floor. These aren't purely decorative: not only do they refer to the brand's logo, but the colour of the dots represents the different price categories in store.

LEFT Long lines, mirrors and the use of indirect light combine to make the most of the 35-m² interior.

FOLLOWING SPREAD Clothing racks were placed between the columns of the 16th-century building to conserve space.

THIS IS NOT JUST A CONSUMER GOOD

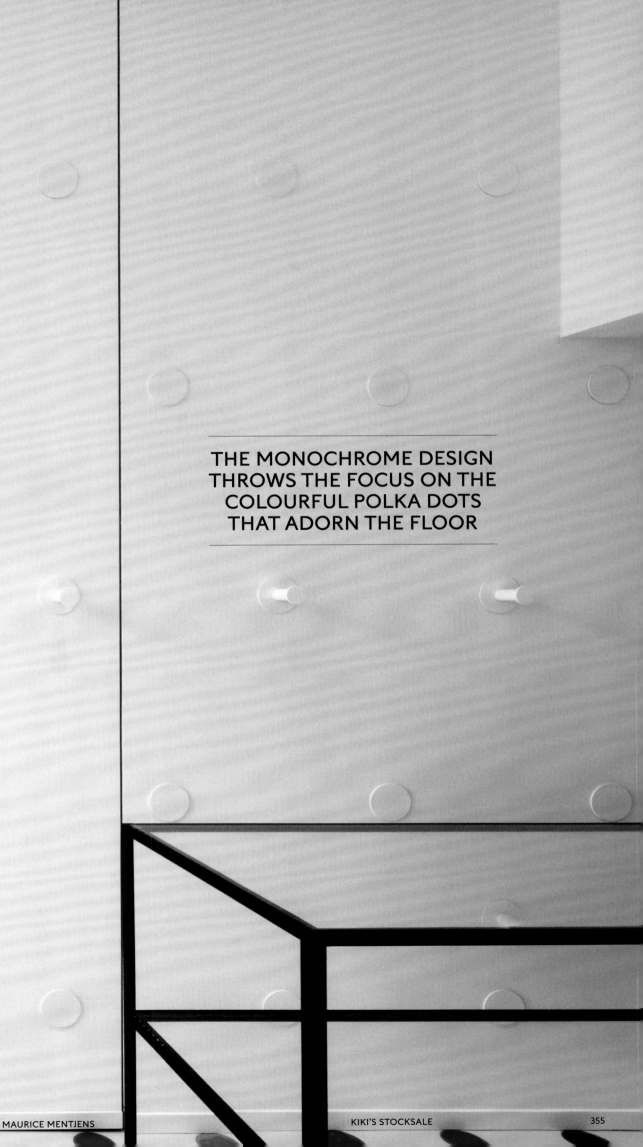

THE MONOCHROME DESIGN
THROWS THE FOCUS ON THE
COLOURFUL POLKA DOTS
THAT ADORN THE FLOOR

Montalba Architects
RAQUEL ALLEGRA

Dominique Vorillon

ABOVE The glass-box changing rooms allow shoppers to take advantage of the generous natural light that fills the shop. They resemble terrariums in the sand-coloured interior and are a perfect fit for the wooden, upholstered furnishings chosen by the client.

RIGHT The shop is long and narrow, but gets copious natural light from the north window and a pair of skylights on each end of the space. A louvered timber ceiling conceals technical equipment.

MONTALBA ARCHITECTS blends contradictions to create a seamless aesthetic in a flagship boutique

LOS ANGELES — The first Raquel Allegra fashion boutique blends 'luxury and comfort, familiarity and exclusivity, detailing and experience,' just like the product it sells, says Montalba Architects. This juxtaposition of contradictory ideas in a 130-m² space determined how the architects thought about the project in general and, more specifically, its materiality. The studio first preserved components of the existing space, and then struck a balance between old and new.

The building enjoys exposure to natural light through the northern facade and two central skylights that bookend the shop. Montalba cleared and opened the retail floor by displaying products along the eastern and western walls and hanging garment racks — in the form of graceful solid brass fixtures — from the ceiling.

The contrast between polished concrete floors and rough stucco walls finds mediation in the choice of refined metal fixtures for hanging clothes and the glass-box dressing rooms lined with thick drapery. Tucked under the roofline, a louvered wooden ceiling emulates heritage structural elements while hiding away unsightly ductwork and electrical wiring. A custom steel storefront window and door were designed in the same language as the rest of the shop, offering clues as to the nature of the brand, the products and the interiors.

Dominique Vorillon

THE CONTRAST
BETWEEN POLISHED
CONCRETE FLOORS
AND ROUGH
STUCCO WALLS
FINDS MEDIATION
IN REFINED
METAL FIXTURES
AND GLASS-BOX
DRESSING ROOMS

LEFT By displaying products along the walls and hanging clothing on solid brass fixtures that loop down from the ceiling, Montalba emptied the centre of the floor, opening sightlines and circulation.

ABOVE From the street, passers-by get a taste of what's inside through a custom-made steel window and door that announce the contents inside.

RIGHT Montalba Architects are known for expressing themselves through bespoke project details like this cast branch door handle at the entrance.

Dominique Vorillon

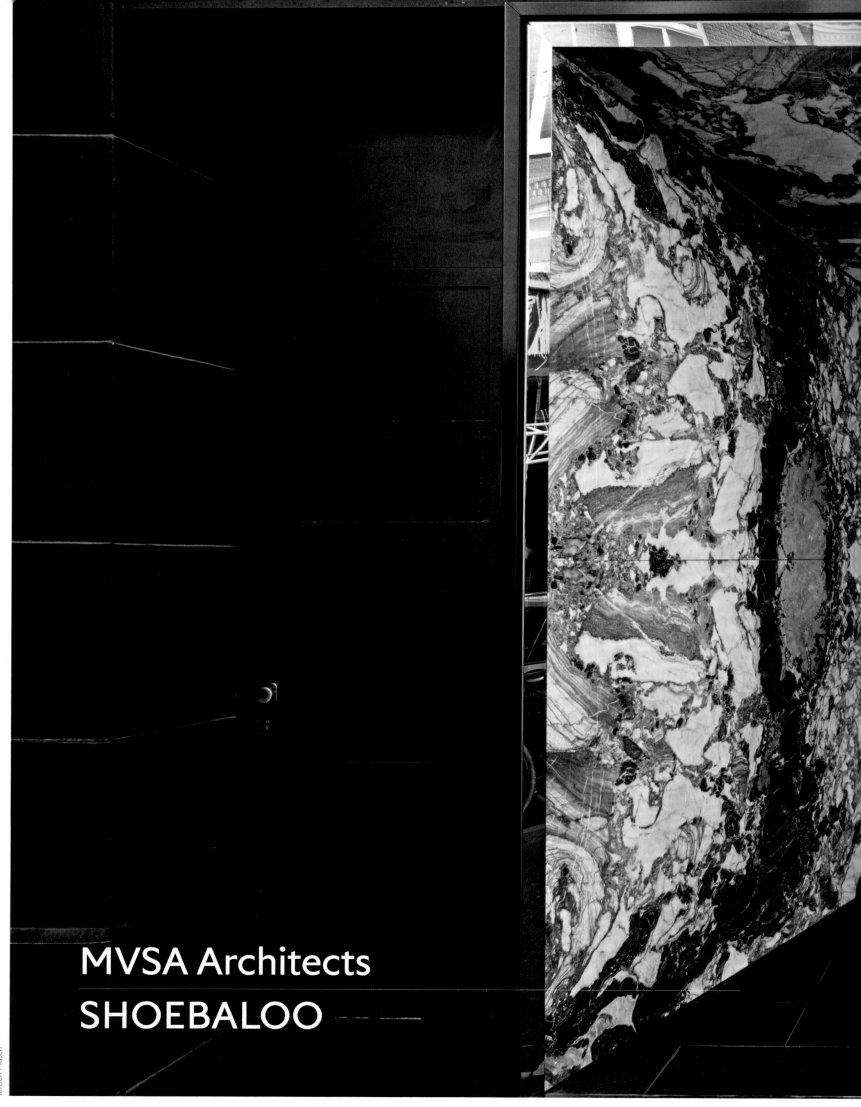

MVSA Architects
SHOEBALOO

MVSA stages a unique customer experience through optical illusions

AMSTERDAM — Shoebaloo is the only store on PC Hooftstraat, the Dutch capital's most prestigious shopping address, without a shop window. Therefore, MVSA Architects had to take a different approach to lure passers-by inside. The international design agency decided to go all out with a grand entrance that uses enormous slabs of Ice Stone marble to not only catch the eye, but play with vision. By mirroring each panel, the natural stone's dark veins and green 'eyes' combine to produce a hallucinatory effect. It's the first of a series of visual tricks that play with perspective. 'Our main goal was to "empower" the shoes by creating an abstract, seductive setting with a large area of display surfaces,' the designers say.

Inside, delicate double-sided louvres seemingly change colour from gold to anthracite as visitors make their way down the corridor. As the upmarket shoes sold here are generally outspoken designs, the subtle colour combination makes them stand out even more. To create yet another illusion, each pair is showcased on translucent sand-blasted shelves that become fully transparent where they meet the walls, so that they appear to float in the air. The customer journey culminates in a glass display at the back of the store, whose mirrors give the impression of extra space and invite customers to turn and continue their quest for the perfect shoe.

PREVIOUS SPREAD Giant slabs of Ice Stone marble more than make up for the fact that this is the only store on the prestigious Amsterdam shopping street with no window.

ABOVE AND RIGHT Double-sided louvres combine to create scenery that appears to magically change from black to golden as the customer moves further inside the store.

THE GRAND ENTRANCE IS THE FIRST OF A SERIES
OF VISUAL TRICKS THAT PLAY WITH PERSPECTIVE

Sibling Architecture
DOT COMME

A fashion archive is given a suitably avant-garde showcase by SIBLING ARCHITECTURE

MELBOURNE — Dot Comme is where fashion collector Octavius La Rosa makes his online collection of avant-garde fashion garments available for sale. As the archive consists of labels including Comme des Garçons, Yohji Yamamoto, Issey Miyake and Walter Van Beirendonck, Sibling Architecture decided to frame these works of art in a gallery-like environment.

Nonetheless, in the same way that the fashion designers listed above subvert stereotypes, the Australian architecture studio created a space where nothing is quite what it seems. Yes, there are white walls, but material-wrapped cardboard tubes have been added to transform their flat surfaces into undulating, bulbous barriers. Some of these tubes conceal the changing rooms, which aren't the only feature lying in wait for visitors.

While some hero pieces are displayed in stainless steel alcoves, most of the clothing is stored behind a door carved into the wall, an insider's reference to the first store of Rei Kawakubo (the founder of Comme des Garçons) in which the collection was concealed in a backroom. The furniture, by Gaetano Pesce, Memphis Milano and Edward Fields, has an equally fabled history. Pesce's table is where customers can use tablets to scroll through the Dot Comme archive and pick out an item, which is then brought out to them from behind the white wall.

LEFT AND BELOW The dimpled stainless steel recesses which host hero pieces also serve to create depth and reflect light.

FOLLOWING SPREAD LEFT Furniture by Gaetano Pesce, Memphis Milano and Edward Fields provides a suitable backdrop to the garments on display.

Sean Fennessy

A SPACE WHERE NOTHING IS QUITE WHAT IT SEEMS

THIS IS NOT JUST A CONSUMER GOOD

Min Chen Xuan

Spacemen
BY

Contrasts and fragments define a highly flexible retail-cum-art-space by SPACEMEN

SHANGHAI — As some retailers abandon their brick-and-mortar presence on the market, e-commerce brands are adding physical stores to their virtual offerings. By's first such location is, pointedly, an experiential space — part retail part art gallery — for a brand with quirky merchandising techniques, like displaying menswear one day and changing it out completely the next, to exhibit pop art, such as character-toy figurines.

Based on this constantly shifting output, Spacemen created a space of contrast and fragmentation built out of materials, shapes and reflections. Angular geometric display alcoves, for instance, are crowned with low-hanging, apparently floating, illuminated ceilings made of stretch Barrisol. Inside these spaces, the floor consists of triangular tiles made of six contrasting types and colours of marble. Their outward facing walls are dressed with angular 8 mm mirrors, camouflaged by reflections of the rest of the room.

At the rear of the 820-m² multi-brand fashion and collectible art shop, the design team made a flexible area for product launches and small fashion shows. Here, an installation of more than 600 recycled plastic shipping pallets can be converted into tiered seating and/or display, being moved and stacked as needed.

PREVIOUS SPREAD By cladding display alcoves with mirrors, a disappearing effect is created which helps bring emphasis to the product within.

BELOW The use of contrasting materials like concrete, marble and textured stucco, was based on the brand's tendency to change merchandising completely at a moment's notice.

RIGHT Tiers of off-white terrazzo can be re-arranged by stacking hundreds of recycled shipping pallets. These form a raised platform that conceals a concrete stump across the store.

Studio David Thulstrup
TABLEAU FLOWER SHOP

　　　　　　　THIS IS NOT JUST A CONSUMER GOOD

FLOWERS TAKE ON A FRESH ROLE, NOT AS WALLFLOWERS OR SUPPORTING ACTORS, BUT AS PROTAGONISTS OF THE SPACE

DAVID THULSTRUP turns a florist into a gallery where flowers are experienced as nature's art and man's design

COPENHAGEN — Local designer David Thulstrup stage set this store, where customers experience flowers in a fresh role — not as wallflowers and supporting actors, but as the protagonists of the 168-m² space. 'It's not only a flower shop,' he says, 'it's an art shop.' Indeed, even the vinyl floor of this floral theater is an artful Yves Klein blue.

Much like a scenographer, Thulstrup began by stripping the walls and ceiling to expose concrete and bricks coarsened over more than a century, exposing textures that represent many histories. By emphasising contrasts of material and texture — rawness with the sleek and glossy — he also juxtaposed the natural and artificial. The designer's floral scenography consists of six tableaux, custom architectural podiums in varying geometric forms and various single materials: terrazzo block, grey glass sheet, transparent glass brick, Bornholm stone, polished metal profiles and perforated metal sheet.

He suspended LED luminaires beneath mirrored metal surfaces that reflect both light and floor and appear to float from the ceiling. On a rack used to aid plant growth, he used various combinations of LED diodes that, during the day, gives off a cool white glow, but overnight looks rosier or even purple. The light helps the plants grow, but for passers-by, it also gives the space the aura of a nightclub.

PREVIOUS SPREAD One large rack helps potted plants to grow, but also serves as lighting and a light sculpture. During the day, this light is white, but overnight it turns to pinkish-purple hue that feels club-like.

LEFT Thulstrup pared back the walls and ceiling to expose old concrete and bricks, surfaces that bear traces of the space's previous occupants going back to the 19th century.

ABOVE The Platonically simple geometric displays showcase extreme textural contrasts as well as the contrast between the man-made and the natural.

Studio MK27
MICASA VOL.C

Fernando Guerra | FG + SG Fotografia de Arquitectura

A light wooden structure by STUDIO MK27 is a beacon for sustainable construction projects

SAO PAULO — Micasa is a furniture store with three buildings: the original store, known as Vol. A; Vol. B, designed in 2007 by Studio MK27 and Vol. C, which the Brazilian design firm was asked to bring to life in 2018. The main requirement for the final piece of this trinity was that it could easily switch functions between its roles as a shop, exhibition space and temporary artist's residence (the latter is made possible thanks to a caravan that fits inside).

The response of designers Marcio Kogan and Marcio Tanaka was informed by the appearance of the other two buildings and a desire to implement the knowledge acquired from the studio's research into the future of construction. The result is a light pavilion with a wooden structural system that the studio believes could lead to a more sustainable and simple form of construction — its detailed joinery allows for quick assembly with zero waste and a low carbon footprint.

Stability is provided by wrapping the wood in translucent polycarbonate for the building's upper half and white metal plate at the base. As to how it relates to its surroundings, Studio MK27 provides a poetic description: 'By contrasting with the "straightness" of Vol.A's metal structure and the brutalist exposed concrete of Vol.B, Vol.C seems to float off the ground gently, like a Japanese lantern.'

FOLLOWING SPREAD LEFT Shadows of the surrounding trees are projected onto the facade during the day to bring the movement of light and nature inside the space.

FOLLOWING SPREAD RIGHT An Isamu Noguchi pendant lamp punctuates Vol. C's double symmetry of the space and explores its vertical dimension.

DETAILED JOINERY ALLOWS FOR QUICK
ASSEMBLY WITH ZERO WASTE AND
A LOW CARBON FOOTPRINT

Superfuturedesign*
THE KAPE

Nothing is what it seems in a modest boutique with hidden depths by SUPERFUTUREDESIGN*

DUBAI — The Kape is a women's fashion brand that specialises in abayas, a loose fitting garment for women that can be worn as either a cloak or dress. Traditionally, these are modest pieces of clothing, but the brand has rewritten the rulebook by introducing colourful prints, intricate adornments and jewellery into its collections. Local studio Superfuturedesign* translated this disruptive attitude into a boutique that, just like an abaya, conceals hidden depths beneath a modest appearance.

A statement of strength is immediately made by the concrete facade that wraps around the store. To take the edge off the rough material, diagonal waves ripple across it to give the appearance of a piece of cloth. Two large windows showcase products, one of which protrudes from the wall to offer another play on perspective.

Once inside, an atmosphere of calm and tranquillity pervades throughout. Sensitive lighting allows The Kape's colourful products to stand out against a clean white background and sleek epoxy resin floor, while earthy pastel tones provide a welcoming touch of warmth. The terracotta tones guide customers towards one more conceptual twist in the fitting room, whose bright scarlet carpet and curtains are a refreshing surprise after the tranquillity established in the rest of the interior.

POWERSHOP 6 THIS IS NOT JUST A CONSUMER GOOD

A BRIGHT SCARLET FITTING ROOM IS A REFRESHING SURPRISE AFTER THE TRANQUIL INTERIOR

PREVIOUS SPREAD The prefabricated cement panels that make up the facade were transformed with a patented moulding technology that produces a wave-like pattern and texture that plays upon the senses.

LEFT A two-tone colour scheme leads customers from the clean product display zones towards the warmer colours found in the changing room.

RIGHT A rich scarlet changing room reveals the disruptive attitude at the heart of the brand.

VALERIO OLGIATI builds a marble-lined canopy that makes shopping feel like lounging in the clouds

MIAMI — This 487-m² flagship in the city's Design District looks as lush as the high-end fashions that are sold inside. Almost the entire two-storey shop — facades, floors, walls, ceilings — has been lined, as if with silk, in a pale blue-green Pinta Verde marble from Brazil. Designer Valerio Olgiati chose this ponderous material for its ability make visitors feel as if they're floating serenely amongst the clouds.

The ground floor of the store is dedicated to exhibitions, while the first floor, at the top of a concrete staircase, showcases the brand's ready-to-wear collections, and features fitting rooms with luxurious floor-to-ceiling curtains. Shoes and handbags are arranged sparsely along minimal shelving without obstructing views of the marble, as well as on low-slung marble podiums and concrete benches that double as display surfaces.

Olgiati envisioned the boutique as a canopy or pavilion supported by concrete pillars, some of which taper to a point just below the ceiling. Pyramids and triangles — tent or canopy-like shapes — feature throughout the store, giving it a sculptural, textural feel. Most visibly, is an acute triangular canopy over the staircase and a four-sided pyramid which emerges from the carpeted floor — both are useless as displays, but are sculptural objects in their own right.

Mikael Olsson

Valerio Olgiati
CELINE

ABOVE A subtly blue-green Pinta Verde
marble from Brazil covers most surfaces of
the store.

TOP RIGHT Poured concrete also appears
in pillars that rise from the building's foundation but at least two of them, one situated
under the stairs, look sculptural, tapering to a
gabled form just beneath the ceiling.

BOTTOM RIGHT The upper floor is where
ready-to-wear clothing and shoes are on
show. In the carpeted area where visitors
try shoes, a pyramid rises from the floor, not
so much as decorative object as an artful
moment.

1ZU33
1zu33.com
info@1zu33.com

Munich-based award-wining studio 1zu33 is an architecture firm working exclusively in the field of spatial brand communication. The studio develops and implements retail concepts, as well as scenography and exhibition design, reflecting brand values in object and material choices. Guided by founders Hendrik Müller and Georg Thiersch, the team of 25 architects and interior designers invests in long-term partnerships with clients like Gaggenau, Aesop, Occhio and Hansgrohe.
p.202, 206

Dennis Lo

A WORK OF SUBSTANCE
aworkofsubstance.com
hello@substance.hk

At the epicentre of Hong Kong's design revolution, A Work of Substance utilises design as a tool to rejuvenate local neighbourhoods, creating works of substance that make the city a place people look to for inspiration. Ever-daring and ever-curious, the practice is constantly venturing into new projects and industries, including the launch of its exclusive line of furniture and lighting. Its work spans the globe from Seoul, Singapore, Bali and Bangkok to Rio de Janeiro and Vancouver.
p.210

Marc Cramer

ÆDIFICA
aedifica.com
info@aedifica.com

Ædifica is a collective of creative professionals and experts from all design fields committed to crafting meaningful, singular and highly valuable places. Delivering award-winning projects across the continent, the firm leverages design intelligence to drive innovation and empower brands, users and communities. From its head office in Montreal, as well as its offices in New York and the Caribbean, Ædifica pools the creative efforts of nearly 200 professionals to the great benefit of its clients worldwide.
p.8, 214

Mark Gong

ALBERTO CAIOLA
albertocaiola.com
office@albertocaiola.com

Alberto Caiola is an award-winning practice specialising in interior, exhibition and product design. Its interdisciplinary thinking reinforces the entire work process, helping the team put forward comprehensive visions that combine a poetic approach with a pragmatic attitude. Through meticulous attention to both process and detail, the practice translates one-of-a-kind narratives into authentic designs.
p.12

ANAGRAMA
anagram.com
hello@anagrama.com

Anagrama was founded in 2009 by Gustavo Muñoz, Sebastian Padilla and Mike Herrera in the northern Mexican city of Monterrey. The trio's idea was to break the traditional creative agency scheme by integrating multidisciplinary teams of creative and business experts. Today, Anagrama employs around 35 people that work for a troupe of international clients from two offices in Monterrey and Mexico City.
p.296

ANDREIA GARCIA ARCHITECTURAL AFFAIRS
andreiagarcia.com
info@andreiagarcia.com

Porto-based Andreia Garcia Architectural Affairs combines architecture with curation, research, design and urban scenography. The studio specialises in projecting architecture into the public consciousness through exhibitions and editorial projects.
p.324

ARCHIEE
archiee.com
info@archiee.com

ARCHIEE is a creative studio founded in Paris in 2011 by Japanese architects Yusuke Kinoshita and Daisuke Sekine. Spanning across disciplines such as architecture, interior design, spatial art and graphics, the duo's creative output is always deeply connected to their architectural ideology and multi-cultural background.
p.100

AREA-17
area-17.com
info.florence@area-17.com

Area-17 Architecture & Interiors is a full service architecture and interior design firm specialising in retail and hospitality. It provides clients with innovative solutions, fulfilling their emotional, aesthetic, operational, and communication goals through an inclusive creative process. Long-time friends with a shared cultural and educational background at the University of Florence, Area-17's partners founded the Florentine office in 2004, and have since opened offices in Hong Kong, Shanghai, Beijing, and Cuenca.
p.104

ARKET
arket.com

An offshoot of Swedish mega-retailer H&M Group, Stockholm-based Arket designs and sells products that are available in several European countries. The young brand describes itself as 'a modern-day market' that offers its own fashion and housewares for men, women and children, but it also curates products by other design-forward brands that contribute to its sophisticated retail mix.
p.216

ATELIER 552
atelier552.com
atelier@atelier522.com

Brand strategy and design firm atelier 522 is always ready to undertake all possible adventures. The studio enjoys exploring new territories with its team of interior, product, graphic and communication designers, architects, communication specialists, business economists, artists, and philosophers. In a truly multidisciplinary environment, these specialists come together to put their energy, knowledge, talent and ideas into designing the things they dream of.
p.108

BARDE + VANVOLTT
barde-vanvoltt.com
hello@barde-vanvoltt.com

Amsterdam-based interior design studio Barde + vanVoltt was launched by Bart van Seggelen and Valérie Boerma in 2014. The duo's mission is to create unique, tailor-made interiors that translate the core values of their clients. Their projects often feature a combination of bespoke furniture, high contrast and brutalist elements. By transforming their client's vision into a space, they tell a story made up of form, colour, materials and narrative elements.
p.16

BATEK ARCHITEKTEN
batekarchitekten.com
contact@batekarchitekten.com

Founder Patrick Batek has been working as an architect since 1999. Based in Berlin, Batek and his team develop architecture, interior and furniture design projects for a widespread client base, including star chef Tim Raue, fashion retailer Zalando, Red Bull and digital agency Razorfish. Preserving the individual atmosphere of spaces is the signature approach of the firm, which specialises in restaurants, bars, hotels, medical practices, offices and private residences.
p.18

BEL EPOK
belepok.com
info@belepok.com

Bel Epok is a design and communication agency consisting of a core team of highly qualified graphic, product and interior designers and communication specialists. Since its foundation in 2001, the studio has maintained a strong focus on luxury and premium consumer goods for brands in the cosmetics, fragrance, fashion and jewellery industries. Its service portfolio spans from consulting and concept development to design and is divided into four distinct units: brand communication, product design, packaging design and retail design.
p.220

BRINKWORTH
brinkworth.co.uk
info@brinkworth.co.uk

London-headquartered Brinkworth is a well-established design consultancy that has worked across the disciplines of architecture, interiors and brand design since opening its doors in 1990. The company has collaborated with other designers and artists, and worked with a range of clients to create a diverse portfolio. The office's client list includes names like Nike, Google, Sonos, Selfridges, Karen Millen, Heineken and The National Gallery.
p.110, 300, 304

BURDIFILEK
burdifilek.com
info@burdifilek.com

Based in Toronto, Burdifilek is an interior design consultancy founded by creative director Diego Burdi and managing partner Paul Filek. Burdi and Filek have designed internationally, partnering with retail, real estate, and hospitality brands for more than two decades. Their approach combines 'sophistication and creative intelligence', seeking inspiration in travel, art and craftsmanship. The resulting expressive interiors transcend trends and engage audiences from all over the world.
p.114, 308

CALVI BRAMBILLA
calvibrambilla.it
studio@calvibrambilla.it

Calvi Brambilla was founded in Milan in 2006 by Fabio Calvi and Paolo Brambilla. Having met at the Polytechnic University of Milan during their undergraduate studies, the two designers went their separate ways before deciding to establish a collaborative studio. A multidisciplinary firm, their work encompasses architecture, interior design and product design.
p.312

CBA CLEMENS BACHMANN ARCHITEKTEN
cbarchitekten.com
info@cbarchitekten.com

Munich-based CBA Clemens Bachmann Architekten was founded in 2004 by Clemens Bachmann. Since its foundation, the office has become known for its wide spectrum of work that ranges from large-scale architectural projects to hospitality interiors and fair booths on a local and international basis. CBA has grown significantly in recent years and currently employs more than ten architects, designers and freelancers.
p.22, 222

CHRISTOPHER WARD STUDIO
christopherward.it
info@christopherward.it

Christopher Ward loves all expressions of design, from product to architecture, but has a particular penchant for fashion, retail and interiors. Ward trained at Politecnico di Milano before working at international studios including Joe Colombo Studio and Duccio Grassi Architects. Based in Reggio Emilia, his studio is composed of a team of young and skilful architects who work on projects all over the world, balancing unconventional material selections and atmospheres into truly creative designs.
p.118, 224

CISZAK DALMAS STUDIO & MATTEO FERRARI
ciszakdalmas.com / matteoferrari.es
info@ciszakdalmas.com

Ciszak Dalmas and Matteo Ferrari is a multidisciplinary team made up of architects and designers based in Madrid. The team aims to work together as a tool to innovate, break barriers and create disruptive concepts, materialising ideas in order to touch, feel and share. The studio works across a range of disciplines including architecture, interior, product design and art direction, using a holistic and experimental approach to devise concepts and services for a wide range of brands.
p.122

CLAUDIO PIRONI & PARTNERS
claudiopironi.archi
info@studiopironi.com

Claudio Pironi & Partners is an Italian interdisciplinary architecture and interior design firm that creates extraordinary experiences across the globe. 'Our philosophy is to design spaces that translate the client's vision into a sequence of emotions forged in materials and geometry, a tale made of uniqueness and poetry,' says founder Claudio Pironi. This tailored approach, attained through a deep knowledge of materials and their potential, aims at creating a unique narrative for every project.
p.126

CLOU ARCHITECTS
clouarchitects.com
info@clouarchitects.com

CLOU is a Beijing-based team of architects led by Jan F. Clostermann and Christian Taeubert. Embracing the multifaceted expressions of contemporary life, the firm's designs revolve around polyvalent spaces. Its clients are partners in endeavours to create contemporary typologies for a rapidly evolving world. By repurposing and recombining, CLOU has the freedom to connect people in new ways and save resources at the same time.
p.228, 316

CORNEILLE UEDINGSLOHMANN ARCHITEKTEN
cue-architekten.de
info@cue-architekten.de

Corneille Uedingslohmann Architekten dedicates itself to comprehensive solutions in the fields of architecture and interior design. Founded by Yves Corneille and Peter Uedingslohmann in 2002, the studio has been working ever since with an emphasis on cultivating long-term relationships with its clients. The practice's portfolio encompasses residential and administrative structures, commercial and public areas, feasibility studies and competitions.
p.130, 134

CREATIVE STUDIO UNRAVEL
studiounravel.com
info@studiounravel.com

Creative Studio Unravel was founded in 2016 by Dongil Lee. At its inception, the Seoul-based practice focused mainly on interiors, but has since flourished into a range of design typologies, from art and architecture to furniture, lighting design and consulting. Unravel continues to design comfortable spaces by honouring their existing conditions instead of working against them.
p.232

CURIOSITY/GWENAEL NICOLAS
curiosity.jp
contact@curiosity.jp

Curiosity was founded by French designer Gwenael Nicolas in 1998. The team of about 25 designers works in a wide range of fields, from retail store concepts and installations, to product and graphic design. Curiosity is based in Tokyo, Japan, but is in constant demand around the world from prestigious clients that trust the firm's unconventional approach to expressing a brand's identity, tradition and appeal.
p.26, 136, 320

DAVID CHIPPERFIELD ARCHITECTS
davidchipperfield.com
info@davidchipperfield.co.uk

David Chipperfield Architects was founded in London by David Chipperfield in 1985. The practice has since won numerous international competitions and built over 100 projects. Offices in London, Berlin, Milan and Shanghai, contribute to the wide range of projects and typologies. Together, the four offices drive common architectural ambitions and share a commitment to the collaborative aspect of creating architecture.
p.30

DFROST RETAIL IDENTITY
dfrost.com
info@dfrost.com

Established in 2008, DFROST Retail Identity is managed by its founders, Nadine Frommer and the brothers Christoph and Fabian Stelzer. More than 50 employees work in inter-disciplinary teams of architects, designers, retail marketing specialists and project managers. Together, they cover a wide spectrum of disciplines, creating tailormade retail experiences that go beyond the norm.
p.34

DIOGO AGUIAR STUDIO
diogoaguiarstudio.com
info@diogoaguiarstudio.com

Diogo Aguiar Studio was founded in 2016 in Porto, Portugal. The architecture studio works at the intersection of design and art, criss-crossing between public and private commissions to create spatial installations and small-scale buildings and interiors.
p.324

DO.DO.
do2.jp
info@do2.jp

Japanese designer Kei Harada founded Do.Do. in 2015 after seven years at Tokyo-based firm Tonerico:inc. Harada's award-wining studio specialises in planning, architectonics and design control for housing, storefronts, offices and exhibits, and develops designs and presentations of furniture and other products.
p.236

EDUARD EREMCHUK
eduarderemchuk.com
info@eduarderemchuk.com

In 2017, architect Eduard Eremchuk founded his eponymous studio. Today its work encompasses different areas of design and architecture. Focusing mainly on commercial and retail interiors, Eremchuk also takes on residential projects. For most spaces, they also design bespoke furniture and decor in which colour, texture and form take a leading role. The studio is currently working with clients in Milan, New York and Moscow.
p.328, 332

FRANCESC RIFÉ
rife-design.com
press@rife-design.com

Interior and industrial designer Francesc Rifé founded his studio in Barcelona in 1994 and currently leads a team of professionals from several design fields. His work is influenced by minimalism and follows a tradition of craftsmanship, focusing on ways of approaching spatial order and geometric proportion, with a special attraction for fine materials. Rifé has received numerous accolades from Contract World, Emporia, Red Dot, FAD and the 8th Ibero-American Biennial CIDI of Interior Design.
p.140

IPPOLITO FLEITZ GROUP
ifgroup.org
info@ifgroup.org

Ippolito Fleitz Group is a multidisciplinary, internationally operating design studio based in Stuttgart. Currently, Ippolito Fleitz Group is a creative unit comprising 80 architects and designers covering a wide range of design territory, including strategy, architecture, interiors, products, graphics and landscape architecture. In 2015, Peter Ippolito and Gunter Fleitz were the first German interior designers to be admitted to *Interior Design* magazine's prestigious 'Hall of Fame'.
p.144

ISORA X LOZURAITYTE STUDIO FOR ARCHITECTURE
ail.lt
info@ail.lt

Lithuanian architects Ona Lozuraitytė and Petras Išora launched Isora x Lozuraityte Studio for Architecture, in Vilnius, in 2014. The two designers have engaged in a number of inter-disciplinary collaborations at a variety of scales, both nationally and internationally. Their wide-ranging commissions revolve around architecture and the arts, encompassing research, archival projects, exhibition and environmental design, private and public space, and urban planning projects.
p.240

ITO MASARU DESIGN PROJECT / SEI
itomasaru.com
sei@itomasaru.com

'Better to be a challenger than a champion' is the belief at the root of Tokyo-based Ito Masaru's work. Dubbed a maverick of the interior design world, Masaru was born in Osaka in 1961 and graduated from Tokyo Zokei University in 1987. Following graduation, he worked for the Kawasaki Takao Office before establishing SEI in 1991. Masaru is currently working on multiple projects in Los Angeles while planning to open a second Japanese office in Kyoto.
p.336

JOHANNES TORPE STUDIOS
johannestorpe.com
info@johannestorpe.com

In 1997, Johannes Torpe launched his namesake studio in Copenhagen. Today, the team has grown to a dozen employees who work across a range of disciplines, from architecture to industrial and interior design. Torpe describes the firm's approach to commissions as 'unrestrained and fearless', and has made the office an advocate for 'creativity without limits'. This risk-taking results in robust concepts and engaging visual storytelling at a variety of scales and in diverse media and markets.
p.340

JSPR
jspr.eu
info@jspr.eu

Eindhoven-based studio JSPR is led by founder and head designer Jasper van Grootel. The team designs distinctive lighting and furniture collections that are produced locally. Their classic products are developed with an eye on the future, and combine creativity with professional craftsmanship.
p.38

JUNYA.ISHIGAMI+ASSOCIATES
jnyi.jp
ji@jnyi.jp

Junya.ishigami+associates is an international architecture firm based in Tokyo, Japan. The office has continued to enjoy growing international attention for its diverse range of projects, from numerous exhibitions and installations, to large-scale commissions. Regardless of scale, the team approaches each project from a limitless and open-ended creative perspective to deliver a unique and inspiring outcome.
p.344

KAPSIMALIS ARCHITECTS
kapsimalisarchitects.com
info@kapsimalisarchitects.com

The work of Santorini-based Kapsimalis Architects flourishes under the influence of the island's coarse volcanic landscape, unpredictable weather, diverse natural materials and ancient architecture. Context, specifically how buildings can be integrated into and contribute to the landscape, is crucial to each project. The architects study the values, customs, time-tested aesthetics and memories of each site and then imbue them with an element of modernity.
p.42

KENGO KUMA
kkaa.co.jp
kuma@kkaa.co.jp

Born in Yokohama in 1954, Kengo Kuma decided to pursue architecture at a young age. He earned his Master's degree at the University of Tokyo's Engineering School in 1979, launched his own practice Spatial Design Studio in 1987, Kengo Kuma & Associates in 1990 and a Paris sister studio 18 years later. The office builds into cultural and environmental contexts, searches for materials to replace concrete and steel and is seeking a new path for architecture in a post-industrial era.
p.348

KNOUBLAUCH
knoblauch.eu
info@knoblauch.eu

Knoblauch was founded in 1909 by Fidel Knoblauch as a small, family-owned carpentry workshop. Three generations later, the company's specialties expanded to shop fitting systems for high-profile retailers like Polo Ralph Lauren. In the last decade, under the auspices of current owner Juergen Zahn, Knoblauch has become an international design studio. With over 200 employees, Knoblauch develops and builds brand spaces in the fields of retail, hospitality and corporate interiors. Clients include Bogner, Marc O'Polo, Freitag and La Prairie.
p.64

KOKAISTUDIOS
kokaistudios.com
info@kokaistudios.com

Kokaistudios is an award-winning architecture and interior design firm founded in 2000 in Venice by Italian architects Filippo Gabbiani and Andrea Destefanis. Since moving to Shanghai in 2002, Kokaistudios has grown into a multi-cultural studio of 60 people working on projects in Asia, the Middle East, Europe and North America. Focusing on developing cultural, corporate, commercial, hospitality and retail projects, the practice has also worked extensively on urban regeneration projects.
p.48, 244

LANDINI ASSOCIATES
landiniassociates.com
press@landiniassociates.com

Landini Associates is a team of 25 designers and strategic thinkers based in Sydney. Established in 1993 by Mark and Rikki Landini, the studio draws on the talents of a strong multidisciplinary team to strategise and design every customer touch point — from buildings to interiors, identities, product and furniture design, graphic communications, way finding, packaging, uniforms, print and digital design — in order to create cohesive and powerful brands.
p.52, 248, 250

LECKIE STUDIO ARCHITECTURE + DESIGN
leckistudio.com
contact@leckistudio.com

Leckie Studio Architecture + Design is an 20-person interdisciplinary design studio that was founded in 2015 by principal architect Michael Leckie. The desire to build a thriving practice that has the capacity to initiate cultural change and architectural innovation was the firm's founding goal. The studio operates with an agenda to expand and evolve traditional models of architectural practice, with work extending across a range of typologies including: modernist single-family homes, multi-family housing, commercial interiors, and conceptually-driven competitions and installations.
p.252

LINEHOUSE
linehousedesign.com
info@linehousedesign.com

Linehouse is an architecture and interior design practice established in 2013 by Alex Mok and Briar Hickling. The practice has international experience in design and construction and works on projects of varying scales and typologies that allow explorations of both poetic ideas and pragmatic solutions. Projects are approached in a holistic manner combining different disciplines and drawing on experience to emphasise quality of construction, detail, materials and light.
p.148, 254

MARCANTE-TESTA
marcante-testa.it
info@marcante-testa.it

Andrea Marcante and Adelaide Testa founded studio Marcante-Testa in 2014. The practice focuses on interior architecture, design and corporate consulting around materials and decor. In 2016, the duo embarked on a collaboration to design interiors in neglected places such as prisons. In their words, their work is simultaneously 'serious and fun, authentic and refined, independent melodies that blend through rigorous rules of composition.'
p.258

MASQUESPACIO
masquespacio.com
info@masquespacio.com

Masquespacio is an award-winning creative consultancy created in 2010 by Ana Milena Hernández Palacios and Christophe Penasse. Combining the two disciplines of their founders — interior design and marketing — the Spanish agency creates branding and interior projects through a unique approach that results in fresh and innovative concepts. Besides its internationally recognised work in interior design, the studio is currently producing its first furniture collections sold exclusively through Masquespacio.
p.152

MAURICE MENTJENS
mauricementjens.com
info@mauricementjens.com

Dutch designer Maurice Mentjens founded his studio in 1990. Based in Holtum, the compact and talented team develops interiors for shops, offices, restaurants, bars, and museum exhibitions. Their aim is to deliver high-end design that reflects their passion. Quality and creativity are prioritised in all aspects of the process, which follows a bespoke approach for each client. The studio's richly layered environments are frequently influenced by the worlds of mythology, history, literature or the visual arts.
p.352

MINAS KOSMIDIS [ARCHITECTURE IN CONCEPT]
minaskosmidis.com
info@minaskosmidis.com

Minas Kosmidis [Architecture in Concept] was established in 2007 in Thessaloniki, Greece. The studio undertakes architecture and interior design projects nationally and internationally. Over the past years, the studio has created a diverse portfolio in the fields of private housing, hospitality and retail, focusing on the sectors of food service and entertainment.
p.154

MONTALBA ARCHITECTS
montalbaarchitects.com
info@montalbaarchitects.com

Founded by David Montalba, this architecture and urban design firm is now made up of four principals and 40 designers. Based in Santa Monica, CA, with a satellite office in Lausanne, Switzerland, the office takes on retail, residential and other commercial projects in a human-centred, socially responsive and aesthetically progressive spirit. Project teams work contextually, approach materials with honesty, express themselves through custom details, and believe that light can animate and change the experience of a space.
p.356

MORIYUKI OCHIAI ARCHITECTS
moriyukiochiai.com
info@moriyukiochiai.com

Tokyo-born Moriyuki Ochiai launched his practice — active in architectural, interior, furniture, landscape and industrial design — in 2008. Ochiai finds inspiration in 'the vivacious beauty of nature,' especially that unique nature enshrined with care and discipline in Japanese temples and gardens. These qualities he interprets and applies to space with sophisticated naiveté, in ways that are simultaneously straightforward and poetic.
p.262

MVRDV
mvrdv.com
info@mvrdv.com

In 1993, Winy Maas, Jacob van Rijs and Nathalie de Vries founded MVRDV in Rotterdam, the Netherlands. Working the world over, the office offers solutions to contemporary architectural and urban questions. With a staff of 250 architects, designers and urbanists, the team's approach is highly collaborative and research-based, a method that draws clients, stakeholders and experts together into the creative process at its inception.
p.158

MVSA ARCHITECTS
mvsa-architects.com
pr@mvsa-architects.com

MVSA Architects is a renowned international architecture and design firm with offices in the Netherlands, Spain and Switzerland. It creates innovative, exciting and future-proof architecture that enhances wellbeing. Its architectural solutions are the result of a collaborative, integrated design approach that embraces the entire architectural process, from first sketch to final detailing. Every design is based on the functional needs of the client, the specific context and the highest standards of sustainability.
p.360

NERI&HU DESIGN AND RESEARCH OFFICE
neriandhu.com
info@neriandhu.com

Established by founding partners Lyndon Neri and Rossana Hu in 2004, Neri&Hu is an interdisciplinary architectural firm. Situated amid the chaotic urban context of Shanghai, the studio views the encompassing city as its muse. With an additional office in London and a team capable of speaking 30 languages, Neri&Hu offers its architecture, master planning, interior and product design services to clients worldwide.
p.56

NIKE DESIGN
nike.com
media.relations@nike.com

Nike Design is recognised as one of the most powerful design houses within a multi-national corporation. John Hoke currently serves as vice president, chief design officer, leading a global team of diverse and fiercely talented designers of every discipline. Hoke completed an MBA at Stanford Graduate School of Business and a Master's in Architectural Design at the University of Pennsylvania. In 2008, he was awarded the permanent title of Alumni Fellow by Pennsylvania State University.
p.60

NONG STUDIO
nong-studio.com
17nong@nong-studio.com

Nong Studio was founded in 2015 by Chasing Wang and Neal Zhu. The team of 20 architects and designers aims to create deep passion and long-lasting richness through their design of interesting spaces. The studio devotes itself to making experiences that will amaze and astonish by finding the balance of different cultures and styles. Nong Studio breaks the boundaries between imagination and design reality, meaning that it is always achieving new possibilities through a human-centred design approach.
p.160

OHLAB
ohlab.net
info@ohlab.net

Helmed by Paloma Hernaiz and Jaime Oliver, Ohlab is a design and architecture studio with a penchant for urban analysis and cultural research. First founded by Hernaiz and Oliver in Shanghai and then relocated to Madrid, the studio is now based in Palma de Mallorca. Whether tasked with the design of a private residence, social housing block, office, shop or museum, Ohlab is equipped to conceive all aspects of a building including, from structure and interior, to its surrounding masterplan.
p.164

OMER ARBEL DESIGN
omerarbel.com
office@omerarbel.com

Omer Arbel Office is the creative Big Bang of a small universe of companies — lighting brand Bocci, among them. The studio is structured to design and execute creative projects of diverse scale and across a broad spectrum of contexts, methods and environments. Based between Vancouver and Berlin, Arbel works deftly in a nebula of architecture, sculpture and design, exploring themes like the intrinsic mechanical, physical and chemical qualities of materials, and experimenting with light as a medium.
p.168

PARTY/SPACE/DESIGN
partyspacedesign.com
info@partyspacedesign.com

Party/Space/Design was formed in 2012 by Suparat Chinathaworn. The firm's services range from interior, exhibition, product and graphic design to architecture, branding and corporate identity, specialising in restaurant and retail interiors. The firm works to ensure that interior design creates a positive effect on the client's business, and society, while exciting the experience of the end user.
p.64

PATTERN STUDIO
patternstudio.net
info@patternstudio.net

Pattern Studio is a dynamic Australian design practice formed in 2016 by Josh Cain and Lily Goodwin. The duo shares a desire to employ design meaningfully, using the built form to create rich, poetic experiences across a range of project typologies. This energetic, progressive team recognises their responsibility to use informed and innovative thinking to sensitively address the complex issues and challenges of today, not only in the context of design and architecture, but on a global scale.
p.170

RIGI DESIGN
rigi-design.com
rigidesign@163.com

Founded in 2007 in Shanghai by Liu Kai, Rigi Design is a growing team of 20 cross-disciplinary designers. The studio's commissions have varied from 'millimetre to kilometre', involving a mix of brand, space, vision, and product design. Kai's philosophy is best described by the motto 'better design, better life' — based on the belief that definitive, clear and warm designs will define our era.
p.266

SCHEMATA ARCHITECTS
schemata.jp
info@schemata.jp

Jo Nagasaka established Schemata Architects immediately after graduating from Tokyo University of the Arts in 1998. Since 2007, the studio has been based in Tokyo from where an ever-expanding expertise covers a wide range of projects from furniture design to architecture in Japan and around the world. Nagasaka's design approach is always based on a 1:1 scale, regardless of the size of the work at hand.
p.174

SCHMIDHUBER

schmidhuber.de
info@schmidhuber.de

Established in 1984, Schmidhuber is a Munich-based design studio that specialises in brand-specific architectural solutions. With a team of over 70 architects and interior designers, the studio implements visionary concepts and moving brand experiences for trade shows, exhibitions, events, shops and showrooms. Openness, respect and reliability are the main pillars of the studio's successful cooperation with its international client base, fostering a refreshing approach to each new project.
p.66

SERGIO MANNINO STUDIO

sergiomannino.com
info@sergiomannino.com

Born and raised in Italy, after graduating from the University of Florence's architecture program, Mannino worked with mid-century design masters Ettore Sottsass and Remo Buti and directed international retail design Studio 63 before launching his eponymous studio in New York in 2008. His multidisciplinary team of architects, interior and graphic designers, and branding consultants specialises in retail, residential, interior, and furniture design for clients like Prada, Miu Miu and Lexus.
p.178, 270

SIBLING ARCHITECTURE

siblingarchitecture.net
sister@siblingarchitecture.com

Sibling Architecture creates environments that make people's lives better through architecture, and design projects that explore all scales and typologies: cultural, commercial, domestic, institutional, urban and landscape. The firm's research-based approach, which includes a passion to explore social needs and desires, strengthens each project with fresh ideas. The practice is directed by Amelia Borg, Nicholas Braun, Jane Caught, Qianyi Lim and Timothy Moore.
p.364

SID LEE ARCHITECTURE

sidleearchitecture.com
mleblanc@sidleearchitecture.com

Sid Lee Architecture is an affiliate of the Sid Lee creative agency, with 600 globally active professionals based in the company's Montreal, Toronto, Paris and Los Angeles offices. Founded in 2009 through the acquisition of the Nomade architectural firm, Sid Lee Architecture is led by architects and senior partners Jean Pelland and Martin Leblanc. The firm offers a wide range of services, from urban analysis and development strategy, to multi-unit residential projects, corporate office design and retail.
p.274

SPACEMEN

spacemen-studio.com
explore@spacemen-studio.com

Founded in early 2014 by Edward Tan, Shanghai-based studio Spacemen is a design firm that specialises in building brand architecture. Its architecture and interior design seizes primary brand strategies and ideologies and transforms them into unique spatial experiences that tell stories. The studio uses emerging technologies to transform static physical spaces into dramatic environments.
p.368

STUDIO AMBER

studioamber.be
info@studioamber.be

Studio Amber is a young Antwerp-based conceptual design firm founded by Amber Feijen in 2017. Feijen's work focuses on the design of spaces and concepts.
p.68

STUDIO DAVID THULSTRUP

studiodavidthulstrup.com
contact@studiodavidthulstrup.com

After stints in the offices of Jean Nouvel and Peter Marino, David Thulstrup opened his studio in Copenhagen in 2009. Since then, he has developed residential architecture and interiors, as well as retail, hospitality and product design together with a diverse team of architects, interior, product and textile designers, 3D visualisers, lighting specialists and materials experts.
p.372

STUDIO DLF

studio-dlf.com
info@studio-dlf.com

Few designers so closely link aesthetics and logic, but for Italy-born, Stuttgart-based Daniele Luciano Ferrazzano, logic seen through an artistic lens lies at the root of the discipline and, especially, at the root of his work. Trained in Germany, his designs reflect a mixture of the rational and functional German Bauhaus with 'the Italian thirst for experimentation'. Ferrazzano launched Studio DLF in 2009. Since then, he has been creating award-winning objects and spaces by balancing simplicity and functionality.
p.72

STUDIO MALKA ARCHITECTURE

stephanemalka.com
contact@stephanemalka.com

Stéphane Malka is an architect, urbanist, theorist, author, lecturer and former graffiti artist. He established Studio Malka Architecture in 2010 in Paris and then opened an office in Los Angeles. Both teams work collaboratively on commissions that vary from residential architecture, office space and retail interiors to scenography, environmental installations and furniture design. Their work is often a synthesis of art and architecture.
p.278

STUDIO MK27
studiomk27.com.br
info@studiomk27.com.br

Studio MK27, located in the chaotic city of Sao Paulo, was founded in the late 1970s by architect Marcio Kogan. Today it is comprised of 30 architects and various collaborators worldwide. The architects of the team, great admirers of the Brazilian modernist generation, seek to fulfil the task of rethinking and giving continuity to this iconic architectural movement. The studio's projects place value on formal simplicity and are elaborated with extreme care and attention to details and finishing.
p.376

STUDIO ROY DE SCHEEMAKER
roydescheemaker.nl
info@roydescheemaker.nl

Amsterdam-based Roy de Scheemaker came to the attention of the design world in 1989 as the author of the rounded multicolour Pallone armchair for Leolux. After working for seven years as a senior designer in another office, de Scheemaker decided to establish his own design studio in 1995. In his work, he collaborates with and assembles multidisciplinary project teams, together with whom he designs high-end private residences and commercial interiors.
p.76

STUDIO XAG
studioxag.com
hello@studioxag.com

A retail design agency launched in 2009 by Xavier Sheriff and Gemma Ruse, Studio XAG specialises in creating 'wow' moments for brands. Today, the team consists of more than 25 designers, makers and forward-thinkers who collaborate on the concept and fabrication of each project. The practice moves fluidly across the fashion, beauty, lifestyle, performance and luxury sectors for brands including Adidas, Calvin Klein and Christian Louboutin.
p.80

SUPERFUTUREDESIGN*
superfuture.design
info@superfuture.design

Superfuturedesign* is a sister studio of ASZarchitetti, founded by Andrea Sensoli, Iacopo Mannelli, Cecilia Morosi and Andrea Rettori. The practice specialises in innovative designs from products to architecture and prides itself on being one of the best firms in the world for 3D visualisation. The brains behind the studio embrace an eclectic ethos to attain a holistic approach. At the same time, they refrain from abiding by current trends and motifs and taking an avant-garde route that is more expressive of their forward-thinking artistic mind-set.
p.182, 380

TACKLEBOX ARCHITECTURE
tacklebox-ny.com
office@tacklebox-ny.com

Jeremy Barbour launched architecture office Tacklebox in Brooklyn in 2006. The studio's work includes retail interiors, commercial office design and single and multi-family residential projects that begin with a study of the history and context of the site. In 2010, Tacklebox was among seven studios selected to receive AIANY's New Practices New York Award. In 2018, *The Architect's Newspaper* ranked the studio among the top 50 interior architecture offices.
p.186

TCHAI
tchai.nl
info@tchai.nl

Tchai is a third-generation family business rooted in China but founded in 1961 by Jan Tchai in Ridderkerk, the Netherlands. Today, granddaughter Kim Tchai heads the office, which seeks 'to find and unlock the Tchi, the vital force, in people and brands alike, by investigating what inspires energy to flow in and around us'. In an increasingly digital and virtual world, the practice animates brands via conceptual thinking, store design, product presentations and other designed experiences.
p.190

UNSTUDIO
unstudio.com
info@unstudio.com

Ben van Berkel studied architecture at the Rietveld Academy in Amsterdam and at the Architectural Association in London, receiving the AA Diploma with Honours in 1987. In 1988, he and Caroline Bos set up an architectural practice in Amsterdam, extending their theoretical and writing projects to the practice of architecture. UNStudio presents itself as a network of specialists in architecture, urban development and infrastructure. The firm has a staff of over 200 creatives from 27 countries, with office locations in Amsterdam, Frankfurt, Shanghai and Hong Kong.
p.84, 88

VALERIO OLGIATI
olgiati.net
mail@olgiati.net

Valerio Olgiati understands his role as an architect who thinks and creates space. He is interested in a non-contextual architecture that emerges from itself. After graduating from ETH in 1986 he lived and worked first in Los Angeles for some years and later in Switzerland. He has taught at various universities, such as ETH Zurich, AA London and Harvard. Today he is a professor at the Accademia di architettura in Mendrisio at the University of Lugano. Since 2008 he runs the office together with his wife Tamara in Flims.
p.384

WATERFROM DESIGN
waterfrom.com
info@waterfrom.com

Established in 2008, Waterfrom straddles the fields of interior design and architecture. Design director Nic Lee, whose work mixes radical simplicity with humour, believes that design should resemble water: simple and pure, organic and ever-changing, essential and full of possibility. The studio's work 'listens' to the story and context of the project in order to create spaces that can convey messages and allow emotions to settle and mature over time.
p.282

WILSON BROTHERS
wilsonbrothers.co.uk
info@wilsonbrothers.co.uk

Wilson Brothers is a creative design partnership formed by London-based siblings Oscar and Ben Wilson in 2006. The brothers have worked in a number of different areas including brand-experience led interior projects and illustration.
p.110

WOODS BAGOT
woodsbagot.com
woodsbagotnewyork@woodsbagot.com

Woods Bagot Global Studio continually expands and challenges the expectations of multi-disciplinary architectural practice in a shifting, fast-moving digital era. Its portfolio is worldwide in scope, diverse in scale and discipline, and encompasses some of the highest-profile projects currently under way in North America, Europe, Asia, Australia and the Middle East. The firm's work is defined by its clarity of narrative and extensive use of state-of-the-art analytics as a platform for design. Above all, Woods Bagot prioritises human experience and delivers engaging, future-oriented projects for its clients.
p.92

YAGYUG DOUGUTEN
yagyug.jp
info@yagyug.jp

Yagyug Douguten is an interior design firm established in Tokyo in 2016 by Fumitaka Suzuki. In 2018, the firm relocated its base to a former tea factory in the mountain village of Nara, and expanded into product design and art installations. By exploring the history and character of people and places, the team breathes a 'story' into its designs. Through this philosophy, the practice aspires to create spaces and products whose stories inspire people to think critically.
p.286

ZELLER & MOYE
zellermoye.com
info@zellermoye.com

Christoph Zeller and Ingrid Moye founded their eponymous architectural studio in Mexico City and Berlin to take an interdisciplinary and global approach to design. Today, the pair works across a broad spectrum of project types and scales, creating anything from furniture to cultural buildings. Ongoing commissions range from residential projects and a public park in Mexico, to memorials in Kurdistan and Berlin.
p.194

ZENTRALNORDEN
zentralnorden.com
ahoi@zentralnorden.com

Four close friends with a passion for graphic design and street art established the Berlin communications and design agency Zentralnorden in 2010. Today, having diversified its array of disciplines, the studio has a staff of more than 20 brand-driven creatives. The team designs concept-based, graphical interiors, thinking of each project as an 'adventurous journey' with their client.
p.290

Index
PROJECTS

004002 – 941, p.216
Copenhagen, Denmark
arket.com

ADIDAS X CONCEPTS, THE SANCTUARY, p.274
Boston, MA, USA
cncpts.com

AESOP NIKOLAISTRASSE, p.202
Leipzig, Germany
aesop.com

ALL SH, p.254
Shanghai, China
allclothingco.com

ANIYE BY, p.224
Noventa di Piave, Italy
aniyeby.com

ANTONIOLUPI, p.312
Milan, Italy
antoniolupi.it

ASSEMBLE BY RÉEL, p.244
Shanghai, China

BAKE CHEESE TART, p.286
Osaka, Japan
cheesetart.com

BILLIONAIRE, p.126
Paris, France
billionaire.com

BROWNS EAST, p.300
London, UK
brownsfashion.com

BROWNS LA POP-UP, p.304
Los Angeles, CA, USA
brownsfashion.com

BULGARI, p.158
Kuala Lumpur, Malaysia
bulgari.com

BY, p.368
Shanghai, China

CAMPER, p.140
Barcelona, Spain
camper.com

CAMPER, p.348
Fidenza, Italy
camper.com

CELINE, p.384
Miami, FL, USA
celine.com

CHA LE MERCHANT TEAHOUSE, p.252
Vancouver, Canada
chaletea.com

CHOCOLATE FACTORY, p.64
Hua-Hin, Thailand

CLAUS PORTO, p.186
New York, NY, USA
clausporto.com

CRYSTALSCAPE, p.262
Tokyo, Japan

DESCENT BLANC NAGOYA, p.174
Nagoya, Japan
descenteblanc.com

DHL EXPRESS, p.190
Amsterdam, the Netherlands
dhlexpress.nl

DOCTOR MANZANA, p.152
Valencia, Spain
doctormanzana.com

DOLCE & GABBANA, p.320
Miami, FL, USA

DOT COMME, p.364
Melbourne, Australia
dotcomme.net

EN, p.100
Paris, France
en-spa.fr

ENGELHORN SPORTS, p.108
Mannheim, Germany
engelhorn.de

ENOTHEK BRIENNER STRASSE, p.22
Munich, Germany

ESSENCE MAKER SHOP, p.34
Berlin, Germany
essence.eu

FIORUCCI, p.110
London, UK
fiorucci.com

FOUR BY AZZURO, p.38
Amsterdam, the Netherlands
fouramsterdam.com

FRIENDS & FRAMES, p.240
Vilnius, Lithuania
fr2.lt

GENTSAC, p.248
Sydney, Australia
gentsac.com.au

GINZA SIX, p.26
Tokyo, Japan
ginza6.tokyo

GLAM SEAMLESS, p.178
New York, NY, USA
glamseamless.com

GUAPA FLOWER SHOP, p.328
Rostov-on-Don, Russia

HARBOOK, p.12
Hangzhou, China

HERSCHEL SUPPLY GASTOWN, p.168
Vancouver, Canada
herschel.com

HERSCHEL SUPPLY SHIBUYA, p.148
Tokyo, Japan
herschel.com

HOMECORE CHAMPS-ELYSÉES, p.278
Paris, France
homecore.com

HUNKE, p.144
Ludwigsburg, Germany
hunke-ludwigsburg.de

IMARIKA, p.258
Milan, Italy
imarika.com

IMMI, p.232
Shanghai, China
immi-fashion.com

IN-SIGHT, p.164
Miami, FL, USA

ISAMU KATAYAMA BACKLASH, p.336
Beijing, China
backlash.jp

JACOB COHËN, p.104
Milan, Italy
jacobcohen.com

JEWELLERY BOX CHAOWAI, p.228
Beijing, China

JINS, p.344
Shanghai, China
jins-cn.com

JIUXI WEDDING EXHIBITION, p.316
Beijing, China

JORDAN STORE, p.8
Toronto, Canada
nike.com

KHROMIS, p.210
Hong Kong
khromis.com

KIKI'S STOCKSALE, p.352
Maastricht, Germany
kikiniesten.nl

KOPPELMANN OPTIK, p.222
Gelterkinden, Switzerland
koppelmann.ch

KULT, p.130
Oldenburg, Germany
kult-olymp-hades.de

LANE 189, p.84
Shanghai, China

LIKESHOP, p.332
Rostov-on-Don, Russia

LITTLE B, p.56
Shanghai, China

MACKAGE, p.114
Toronto, Canada

MAGMODE, p.266
Hangzhou, China
magmode.tmall.com

MAISON BIRKS, p.214
Toronto, Canada
maisonbirks.com

MALABABA, p.122
Madrid, Spain
malababa.com

MASEL, p.182
Milan, Italy
masel.me

MEDLY PHARMACY, p.270
New York, NY, USA
medlypharmacy.com

MICASA VOL.C, p.376
Sao Paulo, Brazil
micasa.com.br

MOLECURE PHARMACY, p.282
Taichung City, Taiwan
molecure.business.site

MONCLER, p.136
Dubai, UAE

MOOSE KNUCKLES, p.308
Toronto, Canada

NAPAPIJRI, p.80
London, UK
napapijri.co.uk

NEW YORK SWEETS, p.154
Nicosia, Cyprus
newyorksweets.com.cy

NIKE HOUSE OF INNOVATION 000, p.60
New York, NY, USA
nike.com

NINGBO ALT-LIFE, p.48
Ningbo, China

NOVELTY, p.296
San Pedro, Mexico

OROVIVO 1856, p.118
Berlin, Germnay
orovivo.de

OVER/UNDER KIOSKS, p.92
New York, NY, USA

ÓYANE SAIKAITOKI, p.236
Hasami, Japan
oyane.jp

PARFUMS UNIQUES, p.206
Munich, Germany
parfums-uniques.de

PRUDÊNCIO STUDIO, p.324
Porto, Portugal
prudenciostudio.com

RAQUEL ALLEGRA, p.356
Los Angeles, CA, USA
raquelallegra.com

SARAH & SEBASTIAN, p.250
Paddington, Australia
sarahandsebastian.com

SHOEBALOO, p.360
Amsterdam, the Netherlands
shoebaloo.nl

SIEMENS SHOWROOM, p.66
Amsterdam, the Netherlands

SKINS COSMETICS, p.76
Rotterdam, the Netherlands
skins.nl

SLTF, p.72
Constance, Germany
soulfoot.de

SNEAKER DISTRICT, p.16
Antwerp, Belgium

SPITZENHAUS, p.220
Zurich, Switzerland
spitzenhaus.com

SPOONING, p.290
Berlin, Germany
spooning-cookie-dough.com

SPORT FÖRG, p.46
Friedberg, Germany
foerg.de

SSENSE MONTREAL, p.30
Montreal, Canada
ssense.com

STUDIO JUSTE, p.134
Cologne, Germany

TABLEAU FLOWER SHOP, p.372
Copenhagen, Denmark
tableau-cph.com

TERMINAL 2 LANDMARK SPACE, p.88
Incheon, South Korea

THE DAILY EDITED, p.170
Melbourne, Australia
thedailyedited.com

THE KAPE, p.380
Dubai, UAE
thekape.com

THE KITCHENS, p.52
Robina, Australia

THE OPEN MARKET IN OIA, p.42
Santorini, Greece

TROQUER FASHION HOUSE, p.194
Mexico City, Mexico

UNITED CYCLING, p.340
Lynge, Denmark
unitedcycling.com

V2 BOUTIQUE, p.160
Shanghai, China

WARRECORDS, p.68
Antwerp, Belgium
warrecords.be

ZALANDO BEAUTY STATION, p.18
Berlin, Germany
zalando.com

Credits
POWERSHOP 6

POWERSHOP 6
NEW RETAIL DESIGN

PUBLISHER
Frame

EDITOR
Ana Martins

AUTHORS
William Georgi and Shonquis Moreno (projects)
Ana Martins (interviews)

DESIGN DIRECTOR
Barbara Iwanicka

GRAPHIC DESIGNER
Zoe Bar-Pereg

PREPRESS
Edward de Nijs

COVER PHOTOGRAPHY
Mikael Olsson

PRINTING
IPP Printers

TRADE DISTRIBUTION USA AND CANADA
Consortium Book Sales & Distribution, LLC.
34 Thirteenth Avenue NE, Suite 101
Minneapolis, MN 55413-1007
T +1 612 746 2600
T +1 800 283 3572 (orders)
F +1 612 746 2606

TRADE DISTRIBUTION BENELUX
Frame Publishers
Luchtvaartstraat 4
1059 CA Amsterdam
the Netherlands
distribution@frameweb.com
frameweb.com

TRADE DISTRIBUTION REST OF WORLD
Thames & Hudson Ltd
181A High Holborn
London WC1V 7QX
United Kingdom
T +44 20 7845 5000
F +44 20 7845 5050

ISBN: 978-94-92311-35-1

© 2019 Frame Publishers, Amsterdam, 2019

Printed on acid-free paper produced from chlorine-free pulp. TCF ∞
Printed in Poland

987654321